Texas Bible English
Level 4
Student Book

For video instructions for each lesson, go to:

www.texasbibleenglish.com

Texas Bible English
Level 4
Student Book

By: Julie Davis
Illustrated By: Chloe Mooring

Copyright © 2020 by Julie Davis.

All rights reserved.

Published in the United States.

Davis, Julie M.
Illustrated by Chloe Mooring

Texas Bible English Level 4 Student Book

Printed in the United States of America.

www.TexasBibleEnglish.com

Scripture quotations marked HCSB are taken from the Holman Christian Standard Bible®, Used by Permission HCSB ©1999,2000,2002,2003,2009 Holman Bible Publishers. Holman Christian Standard Bible®, Holman CSB®, and HCSB® are federally registered trademarks of Holman Bible Publishers.

"Scripture quotations taken from the (NASB®) New American Standard Bible®, Copyright © 1960, 1971, 1977, 1995, 2020 by The Lockman Foundation. Used by permission. All rights reserved. www.lockman.org"

Table of Contents

Lesson 1	Acts	Pages 7-17
Lesson 2	Healing and Encouragement	Pages 18-27
Lesson 3	Giving and Teaching	Pages 28-38
Lesson 4	History	Pages 39-48
Lesson 5	Saul to Paul	Pages 49-59
Lesson 6	Answered Prayer	Pages 60-60
Lesson 7	Sorcery and Assistants	Pages 70-79
Lesson 8	Earthquake	Pages 80-89
Lesson 9	Explaining the Bible	Pages 90-99
Lesson 10	Get Rid of Evil	Pages 100-111
Lesson 11	Heading to Rome	Pages 112-122
Lesson 12	Shipwrecked	Pages 123-131
Lesson 13	The Roman Road	Pages 132-140

Color codes for vowel sounds:

Blue vowels say short sounds:
a apple
e elephant
i iguana
o octopus
u umbrella

Red vowels say long sounds:
a apron
e eagle
i iron
o overalls
u USA

Other color codes:

Purple for silent letters
Green "s" added to words
Yellow for different sound

Color codes for verbs:

Orange root verb present tense
Brown past tense
Gray future tense
Pink past, present, future continuous tense (-ing)
Light blue helping verbs
Dark green past participle

VOCABULARY

Lesson 1

Acts

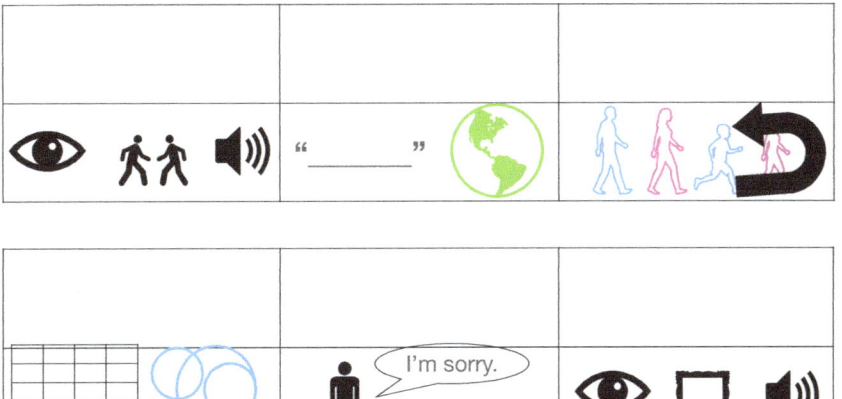

REVIEW WHAT YOU KNOW:

A comma up high	
The last day of the year	
Draw something that we ride in	
What day is Christmas?	

Who? What? Where?	simple, continuous, perfect, perfect continuous	After Jesus went back to Heaven

VOCABULARY

PEOPLE

Instead of practicing words that you already know, you name as many different people as you can without using proper names. Only write the words that someone else says that you don't know or need to practice.

General	Family	Job Titles	Government	At School	At Work
He is a	This is my...	He is the	He is the	She is	He is ...
man					

The Gospels and Acts

Level 3: The stories of when Jesus was here as a man.

All tell the stories from different perspectives of the different followers.

The stories of what the followers of Jesus did after He went back to Heaven.

BIBLE

Acts 1

The Bible says,

1:6 "So when they had come together, they asked Him (Jesus), 'Lord, are You restoring the kingdom to Israel at this time?'

1:7 He said to them, 'It is not for you to know times or periods that the Father has set by His own authority.

1:8 But you will receive power when the Holy Spirit has come on you, and you will be My witnesses in Jerusalem, in all Judea and Samaria, and to the ends of the earth.'

1:9 After He had said this, He was taken up as they were watching, and a cloud took Him out of their sight.

1:10 While He was going, they were gazing into heaven, and suddenly two men in white clothes stood by them.

1:11 They said, 'Men of Galilee, why do you stand looking up into heaven? This Jesus, who has been taken from you into heaven, will come in the same way that you have seen Him going into heaven.'"

Acts 1: 6-11HCSB

In your own words:

1:6 Jesus and His followers were _____. The followers _____.

1:7 _____ said to _____ _____, it is not for you ____ _____… the Father has set by

_____ _____ _____.

1:8 Jesus told them that they would receive _____, they would be _____ in many places.

1:9 Jesus was taken _____.

1:10 The followers were just _____.

1:11 The two men in white said Jesus will _____.

BIBLE | Acts 2

The Bible says,
2:1 "When the day of Pentecost had arrived, they were all together in one place.
2:2 Suddenly a sound like that of a violent rushing wind came from heaven, and it filled the whole house where they were staying.
2:3 And tongues, like flames of fire that were divided, appeared to them and rested on each one of them.
2:4 Then they were all filled with the Holy Spirit and began to speak in different languages, as the Spirit gave them ability for speech.
2:5 There were Jews living in Jerusalem, devout men from every nation under heaven.
2:6 When this sound occurred, a crowd came together and was confused because each one heard them speaking in his own language." Acts 2:1-6HCSB

In your own words:
2:1 After Jesus went back to heaven, on the day of Pentecost, Jesus' followers were _____.
2:2 The loud sound from heaven sounded like a _____.
2:3 Fire that looked like tongues appeared _____.
2:4 When they were filled with the Holy Spirit, they could speak _____.
2:5 There were Jews in Jerusalem from _____.
2:6 They could all hear and understand Jesus' followers in their _____.

`BIBLE`   # Acts 2

The Bible says, at the end of chapter 2, Peter told all about Jesus, and then he said:

2:36 "'Therefore let all the house of Israel know with certainty that God has made this Jesus, who you crucified, both Lord (God) and Messiah (Savior)!'

2:37 When they (the people in the crowd) heard this, they came under deep conviction and said to Peter and the rest of the apostles: 'Brothers, what must we do?'

2:38 'Repent,' Peter said to them, 'and be baptized, each of you, in the name of Jesus Christ for the forgiveness of your sins, and you will receive the gift of the Holy Spirit.'" Acts 2:36-38HCSB

In your own words:

2:36 Peter wanted to make sure everyone knew that God made Jesus _____.

2:37 The people listening were convicted (sorry for their sins) and asked _____.

2:38 Peter said, repent (turn away from your sin) and be baptized (to show faith in) _____

for the _____ of your sins.

Application:

- Do you believe that Jesus is God?
- Do you believe that Jesus came to earth, lived a perfect life, and then returned to Heaven?
- Do you believe that Jesus will come back one day?
- Have you ever repented from your sins and started to follow Jesus?
- Have you ever been baptized to show everyone that you are following Jesus?

LET'S TALK

All About You

1. (Who / Where) (is / are) you from?
2. Who (is / are) in your family?
3. (What / when) (was / is) your favorite color?
4. (Where / when) (is / are) your birthday?
5. (What / when) (is / was) your favorite thing to do?
6. (Where / what) (do / does) you do most days?
7. (How / when) old are you?
8. (How / what) (is / was) your favorite food?
9. (Who / when) (is / are) your best friend?
10. (When / what) time (is / are) it?
11. (Where / what) (is / are) the date? _ _/_ _/_ _ _ _
12. (What / when) (is / are) your name?

WRITING

Describe People

Describe what you see in this picture.

Include colors, facial expressions, numbers, and backgrounds.

Irregular Verbs & Past Participles

FILL IN THE BLANKS

MAIN VERB	← PAST	↓ PRESENT	→ FUTURE	Have/Has/Had	PAST PARTICIPLE
accept			will / going to	Have/Has/Had	
achieve			will / going to	Have/Has/Had	
admit			will / going to	Have/Has/Had	
advise			will / going to	Have/Has/Had	
address			will / going to	Have/Has/Had	
agree			will / going to	Have/Has/Had	
answer			will / going to	Have/Has/Had	
attract			will / going to	Have/Has/Had	
apologize			will / going to	Have/Has/Had	
apply			will / going to	Have/Has/Had	

I / we / you / they — have
he / she / it — has

I / we / you / they / he / she / it — had

FILL IN THE BLANKS	PAST	PRESENT	FUTURE

VERB: ACCEPT

SIMPLE

PAST
+ed, new word, did not, did?
(I,we,you,they)(he,she,it)

1. ____ _____ the offer.
2. ___ ___ ___ _____ the offer.
3. ___ ____ _____ the offer?

PRESENT
verb, +s,es, do not, do?
(I,we,you,they)(he,she,it)

1. ____ _____ the offer.
2. ___ ___ ____ _____ the offer.
3. ___ _____ _____ the offer?

FUTURE
will, will not, will?
(I,we,you,they)(he,she,it)

1. _____ _____ the offer.
2. _____ ___ ___ _____ the offer.
3. ____ _____ _____ the offer?

CONTINUOUS

+ing = action continues for a time

PAST
was, were, +ing, not, ?
(we,you,they)(I,he,she,it)

1. _____ _____ the offer.
2. _____ _____ ___ _____ the offer.
3. _____ ____ _____ the offer?

PRESENT
am,is,are, not, ?
(I)(we,you,they)(he,she,it)

1. _____ _____ the offer.
2. _____ _____ ___ _____ the offer.
3. _____ _____ _____ the offer?

FUTURE
will be, will not be, will ?
(we,you,they)(I,he,she,it)

1. _____ _____ the offer.
2. _____ ___ ___ ___ the offer.
3. _____ ___ _____ the offer?

PERFECT

had,have,has,will have PP
actions completed in past, but relates to another time

PAST
had, had PP, not PP, had PP?
(we,you,they)(I,he,she,it)

1. ____ ____ _____ the offer.
2. _____ ____ ___ ___ the offer.
3. ___ ____ _____ the offer?

PRESENT
have, has PP, not PP, PP?
(I,we,you,they)(he,she,it)

1. _____ ____ _____ the offer.
2. _____ ____ _____ the offer.
3. _____ _____ _____ the offer?

FUTURE
will have PP, will not have PP, PP?
(I,we,you,they)(he,she,it)

1. _____ _____ the offer.
2. _____ ___ ___ _____ the offer.
3. _____ _____ _____ the offer?

PERFECT CONTINUOUS

+had,have,has been
completed, but will continue

PAST
had been +ing, had not been +ing, Had __ +ing?
(we,you,they)(I,he,she,it)

1. _____ _____ _____ _____ the offer.
2. _____ _____ _____ _____ the offer.
3. _____ _____ _____ _____ the offer?

PRESENT
have, has been +ing, not been +ing, been +ing?
(I,we,you,they)(he,she,it)

1. _____ _____ _____ the offer.
2. ___ ___ ___ _____ the offer.
3. ___ ___ ___ ___ the offer?

FUTURE
will have been +ing, will not, +ing?
(I,we,you,they)(he,she,it)

1. _____ _____ _____ the offer.
2. _____ ___ ___ _____ the offer.
3. ___ ___ ___ _____ the offer?

MOVIES, MUSIC, LESSONS

EXTRA HOMEWORK: Watch the movie *The Pistol*. Follow the YouTube link on the website: www.texasbibleenglish.com on Level 4, Lesson 1 Set the subtitles to your language so you can understand the story. Answer these questions.

Movie Review Questions:

1. What was your favorite part of the movie?
2. Who in his family helped Pete become a great basketball player?
3. Why did Pete have to work harder than some of the other players on the team?
4. Who was nice to Pete at school?
5. What happened at the end of the movie?

VOCABULARY

Lesson 2

Healing and Encouragement

REVIEW WHAT YOU KNOW:

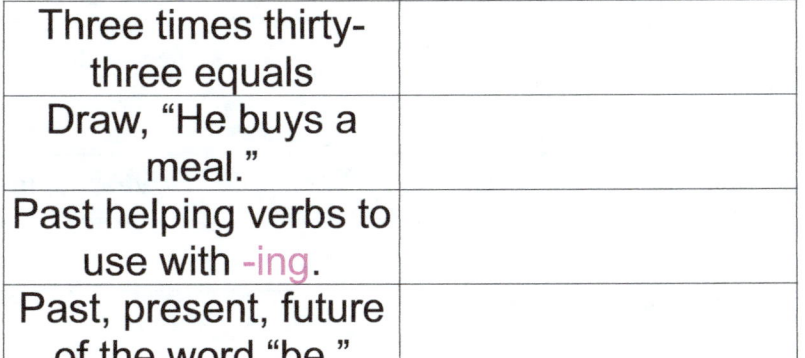

Three times thirty-three equals	
Draw, "He buys a meal."	
Past helping verbs to use with -ing.	
Past, present, future of the word "be."	

VOCABULARY

ADJECTIVES

Adjectives describe a noun (person, place, thing) and usually are after the noun.

Best-Friend	Children	Parents	Bosses or Teachers	spouse	pets

`BIBLE`

Acts 3

The Bible says,

3:1 "Now Peter and John were going up together to the temple complex at the hour of prayer at three in the afternoon.

3:2 And a man who was lame from birth was carried there and placed every day at the temple gate called Beautiful, so he could beg from those entering the temple complex.

3:3 When he saw Peter and John about to enter the temple complex, he asked for help.

3:4 Peter, along with John, looked at him intently and said, 'Look at us.'

3:5 So he turned to them, expecting to get something from them.

3:6 But Peter said, 'I don't have silver or gold, but what I have, I give you: In the name of Jesus Christ the Nazarene, get up and walk!'

3:7 Then, taking him by the right hand he raised him up, and at once his feet and ankles became strong.

3:8 So he jumped up, stood, and started to walk, and he entered the temple complex with them - walking, leaping, and praising God.

3:9 All the people saw him walking and praising God…" Acts 3:1-10 HCSB

In your own words:

3:5 The lame man thought Peter and John were going to give him _____.

3:6 The man was healed by the name of _____.

3:7 The man started _____.

BIBLE

Acts 4

The Bible says,
4:8 "Then Peter was filled with the Holy Spirit and said to them, 'Rulers of the people and elders:
4:9 If we are being examined today about a good deed done to a disabled man - by what means he was healed -
4:10 let it be known to all of you and to all the people of Israel, that by the name of Jesus Christ the Nazarene - whom you crucified and whom God raised from the dead - by Him this man is standing here before you healthy.
4:11 This Jesus is the stone rejected by you builders, which has become the cornerstone.
4:12 There is salvation in no one else, for there is no other name under heaven given to people, and we must be saved by it.'" Acts 4:8-12HCSB

In your own words:
4:10 The lame man was healed by _____.
4:12 Peter made it very clear that they only way to be saved from our sins is by _____

 **BIBLE**   # Acts 4

The Bible says:

4:32 "Now the large group of those who believed were of one heart and mind, and no one said that any of his possessions was his own, but instead they held everything in common.

4:33 And the apostles were giving testimony with great power to the resurrection of the Lord Jesus, and great grace was on all of them.

4:34 For there was not a needy person among them, because all those who owned lands or houses sold them, brought the proceeds of the things that were sold,

4:35 and laid them at the apostles' feet. This was then distributed for each person's basic needs.

4:36 Joseph, a Levite and a Cypriot by birth, the one the apostles called Barnabas, which is translated Son of Encouragement,

4:37 sold a field he owned, brought the money, and laid it at the apostles' feet." Acts 4:32-37HCSB

In your own words:

4:32 The believers and followers of Jesus were unified and cared more about each other than _____.

4:33 The apostles were _____.

4:34 The people were not needy because _____.

Application:

- These chapters are about giving. Do you give Jesus what He has given you? Time? Money? Resources?
- Do you give people the truths that you know about Jesus?
- Do you enjoy giving things you have to people in need?

LET'S TALK Schedule

Find today on the calendar and answer the questions:

1. What are you doing tomorrow?
   _____
2. What did you do this Monday?
   _____
3. What did you do last weekend?
   _____
4. When is your doctor's visit?
   _____
5. What might you do this weekend?
   _____
6. When do you do your grocery shopping?
   _____
7. When did you paint your house?
   _____
8. What are you doing today?
   _____
9. What days are you free?
   _____

Describe

WRITING

24

FILL IN THE BLANKS **Irregular Verbs & Past Participles**

MAIN VERB	← PAST	↓ PRESENT	→ FUTURE	Have/Has/Had	PAST PARTICIPLE
be			will / going to	Have/Has/Had	
become			will / going to	Have/Has/Had	
begin			will / going to	Have/Has/Had	
behave			will / going to	Have/Has/Had	
bite			will / going to	Have/Has/Had	
breathe			will / going to	Have/Has/Had	
build			will / going to	Have/Has/Had	
burn			will / going to	Have/Has/Had	
believe			will / going to	Have/Has/Had	
bless			will / going to	Have/Has/Had	

I / we / you / they — have
he / she / it — has

I / we / you / they / he / she / it — had

FILL IN THE BLANKS

VERB: BELIEVE

SIMPLE

+ing = action continues for a time

CONTINUOUS

had,have,has,will have PP
actions completed in past, but relates to another time

PERFECT

+had,have,has been
completed, but will continue

PERFECT CONTINUOUS

PAST	PRESENT	FUTURE
am,is,are, am,is,are not, Are? (I,we,you,they)(he,she,it) 1. ____ _____ the Bible. 2. ___ _____ ___ the Bible. 3. ___ ____ in Bible?	verb, +s,es,do not, do? (I,we,you,they)(he,she,it) 1. ____ _____ the Bible. 2.____ _____ ___ _____ the Bible. 3. _____ ____ _____ the Bible?	will, will not, will? (I,we,you,they)(he,she,it) 1. _____ ___ ____ the Bible. 2. _____ _____ _____ the Bible. 3. ____ _____ ____ the Bible?
was, were, +ing, not, ? (we,you,they)(I,he,she,it) 1. _____ ____ _____ the Bible. 2. ____ ____ ___ _____ the Bible. 3. _____ ____ _____ the Bible?	am,is,are, +ing, not +ing, +ing ? (I)(we,you,they)(he,she,it) 1. _____ ____ _____ the Bible. 2._____ _____ ___ _____ the Bible. 3. _____ ____ _____ the Bible?	will be, will not be, will ? (we,you,they)(I,he,she,it) 1. ____ ____ ____ _____the Bible. 2._____ ____ _____ _____ the Bible. 3. ____ _____ _____ the Bible?
had, had PP, not PP, had PP? (we,you,they)(I,he,she,it) 1.____ ____ _____the Bible 2._____ ____ ___ _____ the Bible. 3. ___ _____ _____ the Bible?	have, has PP, not PP, PP? (I,we,you,they)(he,she,it) 1. _____ _____ _____ the Bible. 2. _____ ___ ___ _____ the Bible 3. _____ _____ _____ the Bible?	will have PP, will not have PP, PP? (I,we,you,they)(he,she,it) 1._____ ____ _____ the Bible. 2._____ _____ ____ _____ the Bible. 3. _____ _____ the Bible?
had been +ing, had not been +ing, Had __ +ing? (we,you,they)(I,he,she,it) 1. _____ ____ _____ _____ the Bible. 2. _____ _____ _____ _____ the Bible 3. _____ ____ _____ ____ _____ the Bible?	have, has been +ing, not been +ing, been +ing? (I,we,you,they)(he,she,it) 1. _____ ____ _____ _____ the Bible. 2. ____ ____ _____ _____ the Bible 3. ____ _____ _____ _____ the Bible?	will have been +ing, will not, +ing? (I,we,you,they)(he,she,it) 1. ____ ____ _____ _____ the Bible. 2.____ _____ _____ ____ _____ the Bible. 3. ____ _____ _____ ____ the Bible?

EXTRA HOMEWORK: Watch the movie *Courageous*. Set the subtitles to your language so you can understand the story. Answer these questions.

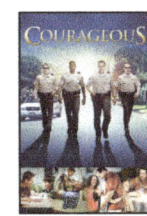

Movie Review Questions:

1. What was your favorite part of the movie?

2. What did Adam's daughter want him to do?

3. What happened to make Adam want to be a better father?

4. What did Havier believe that God would do?

5. What happened to Nathan's truck and baby at the beginning of the movie?

VOCABULARY

Lesson 3

Giving and Teaching

REVIEW WHAT YOU KNOW:

Where we go when we are very sick.	
Draw something for the fall season.	
What is the opposite of happy?	
One less than one million	

PLACES

Name as many places as you can for each category

In a city	In a school	At work	Outside	In a house	For vacation

BIBLE

Acts 5

The Bible says,

5:1 "But a man named Ananias, with his wife Sapphira, sold a piece of property.

5:2 However, he kept back part of the proceeds with his wife's knowledge, and brought a portion of it and laid it at the apostles' feet.

5:3 Then Peter said, 'Ananias, why has Satan filled your heart to lie to the Holy Spirit and keep back part of the proceeds from the field?

5:4 Wasn't it yours while you possessed it? And after it was sold, wasn't it at your disposal? Why is it that you planned this thing in your heart? You have not lied to men but to God!'

5:5 When he heard these words, Ananias dropped dead, and a great fear came on all who heard.

5:6 The young men got up, wrapped his body, carried him out, and buried him.

5:7 There was an interval of about three hours; then his wife came in, not knowing what had happened.

5:8 'Tell me,' Peter asked her, 'Did you sell the field for this price?' 'Yes,' she said, 'for that price.'

5:9 Then Peter said to her, 'Why did you agree to test the Spirit of the Lord? Look! The feet of those who have buried your husband are at the door, and they will carry you out!'

5:10 Instantly she dropped dead at his feet. When the young men came in, they found her dead, carried her out, and buried her beside her husband." Acts 5:1-10 HCSB

In your own words:

5:4 The couple had the land and could do what they wanted, but they decided to _____

5:4 They did not lie to _____ but _____.

5:7 Three hours after Ananias died, _____.

5:8 Peter asked her, _____. She said, _____

`BIBLE`

Acts 5

The Bible says,
5:12 "Many signs and wonders were being done among the people through the hands of the apostles…"
5:14 "Believers were added to the Lord in increasing numbers - crowds of both men and women."
5:17 "Then the high priest took action. He and all his colleagues, those who belonged to the party of the Sadducees, were filled with jealousy.
5:18 So they arrested the apostles and put them in the city jail.
5:19 But an angel of the Lord opened the doors of the jail during the night, brought them out, and said,
5:20 'Go and stand in the temple complex, and tell the people all about this life.'
5:21 In obedience to this, they entered the temple complex at daybreak and began to teach.
5:25 Someone came and reported to them (the religious leaders), 'Look! The men you put in jail are standing in the temple complex and teaching the people.'
5:26 Then the commander went with the temple police and brought them in without force, because they were afraid the people might stone them." Acts 5:12,14,17-26HCSB

In your own words:
5:17 The hight priest and other religious leaders were filled with _____.
5:19 In the night and angel of the Lord _____.
5:21 Peter and John were not afraid. As soon as they got out of jail they _____.

| BIBLE | Acts 5 |

The Bible says,

5:27 "After they brought them in, they had them stand before the Sanhedrin, and the high priest asked,

5:28 'Didn't we strictly order you not to teach in this name? And look, you have filled Jerusalem with your teaching and are determined to bring this man's blood on us!'

5:29 But Peter and the apostles replied, 'We must obey God rather than men.

5:30 The God of our fathers raised up Jesus, whom you had murdered by hanging Him on a tree.

5:31 God exalted this man to His right hand as ruler and Savior, to grant repentance to Israel, and forgiveness of sins.

5:32 We are witnesses of these things, and so is the Holy Spirit whom God has given to those who obey Him."

5:40 After they called in the apostles and had them flogged (beat them), they ordered them not to speak in the name of Jesus and released them.

5:41 Then they went out from the presence of the Sanhedrin, rejoicing that they were counted worthy to be dishonored on behalf of the Name.

5:42 Every day in the temple complex, and in various homes, they continued teaching and proclaiming the good news that Jesus is the Messiah." Acts 5:27-32,41-42HCSB

In your own words:

5:29 The followers of Jesus were determined to obey _____.

5:30 They told the story again of how God _____.

5:31 They reminded everyone that Jesus is the Savior Who _____.

5:41 They did not get angry after they were beaten, but instead they _____.

5:42 They did not stop _____.

BIBLE

Acts 6

The Bible says:
6:2 Then the Twelve (disciples) summoned the whole company of the disciples and said, 'It would not be right for us to give up preaching about God to handle financial matters.
6:3 Therefore, brothers, select from among you seven men of good reputation, full of the Spirit and wisdom, whom we can appoint to this duty.
6:4 But we will devote ourselves to prayer and to the preaching ministry.'
6:5 The proposal pleased the whole company. So they chose Stephen, a man full of faith and the Holy Spirit, and Philip, Prochorus, Nicanor, Timon, Parmesan, and Nicolaus, a proselyte from Antioch.
6:6 They had them stand before the apostles who prayed and laid their hands on them.
6:7 So the preaching about God flourished, the number of the disciples in Jerusalem multiplied greatly, and a large group of priests became obedient to the faith." Acts 6:2-7HCSB

In your own words:
6:2 The disciples had a lot of work to do, but they didn't want to stop preaching, so they _____
6:3 The men selected to help had to be _____.

Application:
- Have you decided to obey God instead of people?
- How would you feel if you were punished just because you believed in Jesus?
- Do you sometimes think about how you can serve God like these disciples and followers?

LET'S TALK

How Long?

1. How long have you been driving?

2. How long have you been taking English classes?

3. How long will you be working?

4. How long have you been a parent?

5. How long will you be sleeping tonight?

6. How long have you been married?

7. How long have you lived in your home?

8. How long does it take you to get from your house to the grocery store?

9. How long does it take you to get ready each morning?

10. How long is the wait at your barber shop?

WRITING

Describe

FILL IN THE BLANKS	Irregular Verbs & Past Participles				

MAIN VERB	← PAST	PRESENT ↓	→ FUTURE	Have Has Had	PAST PARTICIPLE
call			will going to	Have Has Had	
capture			will going to	Have Has Had	
carry			will going to	Have Has Had	
catch			will going to	Have Has Had	
choose			will going to	Have Has Had	
cough			will going to	Have Has Had	
cut			will going to	Have Has Had	
crash			will going to	Have Has Had	
cross			will going to	Have Has Had	
counsel			will going to	Have Has Had	

I
we
you
they   have

he
she
it   has

I
we
you
they   had

he
she
it

FILL IN THE BLANKS

VERB: CALL

	PAST	PRESENT	FUTURE
SIMPLE	+ed, new word, did not, did? (I,we,you,they)(he,she,it) 1. ____ _____ the police. 2. ___ ___ _____ _____ the police. 3. ___ ___ _____ the police?	verb, +s,es, do not, do? (I,we,you,they)(he,she,it) 1. ____ _____ the police. 2. ___ ___ ___ _____ the police. 3. ___ ___ _____ the police?	will, will not, will? (I,we,you,they)(he,she,it) 1. ____ _____ the police. 2. ___ ____ _____ the police. 3. ____ _____ the police?
CONTINUOUS +ing = action continues for a time	was, were, +ing, not, ? (we,you,they)(I,he,she,it) 1. _____ _____ the police. 2. _____ ___ _____ the police. 3. _____ ____ _____ the police?	am, is, are, not, ? (I)(we,you,they)(he,she,it) 1. _____ _____ the police. 2. _____ _____ ___ _____ the police. 3. _____ _____ _____ the police?	will be, will not be, will ? (we,you,they)(I,he,she,it) 1. _____ _____ the police. 2. _____ _____ ___ _____ the police 3. _____ ___ _____ the police?
PERFECT had, have, has, will have PP actions completed in past, but relates to another time	had, had PP, not PP, had PP? (we,you,they)(I,he,she,it) 1. ____ ____ _____ the police. 2. ____ ___ _____ the police. 3. ___ ____ _____ the police?	have, has PP, not PP, PP? (I,we,you,they)(he,she,it) 1. ____ ____ _____ the police. 2. ____ ____ _____ the police. 3. ____ ___ _____ the police?	will have PP, will not have PP, PP? (I,we,you,they)(he,she,it) 1. _____ _____ the police. 2. _____ _____ the police. 3. _____ _____ the police?
PERFECT CONTINUOUS +had,have,has been completed, but will continue	had been +ing, had not been +ing, Had __ +ing? (we,you,they)(I,he,she,it) 1. ____ _____ the police. 2. ____ _____ _____ the police. 3. ____ ____ _____ the police?	have, has been +ing, not been +ing, been +ing? (I,we,you,they)(he,she,it) 1. ___ ____ _____ the police. 2. ___ ___ _____ _____ the police. 3. ___ ___ _____ _____ the police?	will have been +ing, will not, +ing? (I,we,you,they)(he,she,it) 1. _____ _____ the police. 2. _____ _____ the police. 3. _____ _____ the police?

EXTRA HOMEWORK: Watch the movie *Fireproof.* Set the subtitles to your language so you can understand the story. Answer these questions.

Movie Review Questions:

1. What was your favorite part of the movie?
2. What was Caleb saving money for?
3. How did Caleb trick Wayne when he drank the hot sauce?
4. What changed Caleb to be able to love his wife?
5. How did Caleb's parents help him save his marriage?

Lesson 4

History

REVIEW WHAT YOU KNOW:

Draw 5 triangles and 3 ovals.	
How many hours are in a day?	
What is the name of the last book of the Bible?	
What are you doing?	

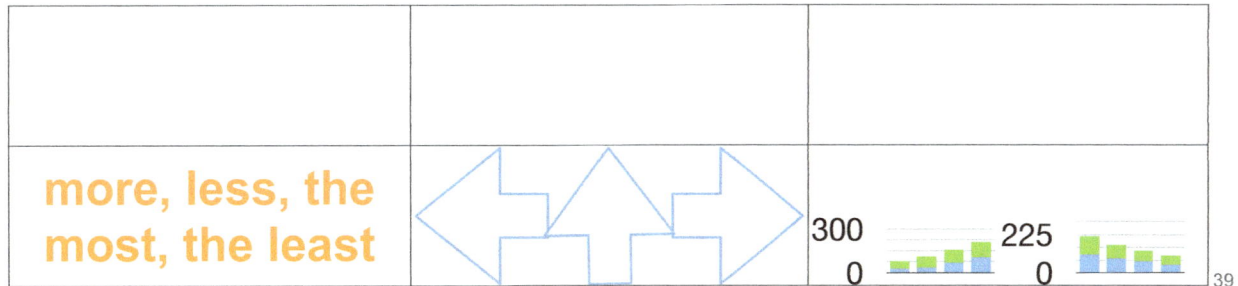

more, less, the most, the least

VOCABULARY

Things

Name as many things as you can for each category

At home	At school	At work	Foods	Vehicles	Things you wear

Acts 6 - 7

The Bible says,
6:8 "Stephen, full of grace and power, was performing great wonders and signs among the people.
6:9 Then some from what is called the Freedmen's Synagogue, composed of both Cyrenians and Alexandrians, and some from Cilicia and Asia, came forward and disputed with Stephen.
6:10 But they were unable to stand up against his wisdom and the Spirit by whom he was speaking.
7:2 'Brothers and fathers,' he said, 'listen: The God of glory appeared to our father Abraham…
7:5 He didn't give him an inheritance in it, not even a foot of ground, but He promised to give it to him as a possession, and to his descendants after him, even though he was childless.
7:9 The patriarchs became jealous of Joseph and sold him into Egypt, but God was with him
7:10 and rescued him out of all his troubles.
7:17 As the time was drawing near to fulfill the promise that God had made to Abraham, the people flourished and multiplied in Egypt
7:18 until a different king who did not know Joseph ruled over Egypt.
7:19 He dealt deceitfully with our race and oppressed our ancestors by making them leave their infants outside, so they wouldn't survive." Acts 6:8-10; 7:5,9,10,17-19 HCSB

In your own words:
7:2 Stephen started reminding the people about how God always saved His people. He started with the story of _____.
7:9 He continued with the story of Joseph and how God _____.
7:18-19 Things got hard again for God's people because _____.

| BIBLE |

Acts 7

The Bible says,

7:20 "At this time Moses was born, and he was beautiful in God's sight.

7:30 After 40 years had passed, an angel appeared to him in the wilderness of Mount Sinai, in the flame of a burning bush.

7:36 This man led them out and performed wonders and signs in the land of Egypt, at the Red Sea, and in the wilderness 40 years.

7:45 Our ancestors in turn received it and with Joshua brought it in when they dispossessed the nations that God drove out before our fathers, until the days of David.

7:46 He found favor in God's sight and asked that he might provide a dwelling place for the God of Jacob.

7:47 But it was Solomon who built Him a house.

7:51 You stiff-necked people with uncircumcised hearts and ears! You are always resisting the Holy Spirit; as your ancestors did, so do you.

7:54 When they heard these things, they were enraged in their hearts and gnashed their teeth at him.

7:59 They were stoning Stephen as he called out: 'Lord Jesus, receive my spirit!'"

Acts 7:20,30,36,45-47,51,54,59 HCSB

In your own words:

7:30 Stephen reminded them of the story of when God spoke to Moses at the _____

7:36 He reminded them of the wonders like the Red Sea when God _____.

7:45 He mentioned the story of Joshua (and the wall of Jericho) when God _____.

7:47 The temple was built by _____.

7:59 Stephen told the people the truth of the Bible and they _____.

BIBLE

Acts 8

The Bible says,
8:1 "Saul agreed with putting him (Stephen) to death. On that day a severe persecution broke out against the church in Jerusalem and all except the apostles were scattered throughout the land of Judea and Samaria.
8:2 Devout men buried Stephen and mourned deeply over him.
8:3 Saul, however, was ravaging the church. He would enter house after house, drag off men and women, and put them in prison.
8:4 So those who were scattered went on their way preaching the message of good news." Acts 8:1-4 HCSB

In your own words:
8:1 Saul _____. That day started very bad _____.
8:3 Saul was _____.
8:4 The believers that had to leave their houses went on _____.

Application:
- Stephen reminded the people of how God saves those who believe Him. God is always faithful. How has God saved or helped you?
- Stephen was killed and many believers lost their homes and all they owned just because they followed the teachings of Jesus. Would you be willing to lose everything for what you believed?

LET'S TALK

Superlative = the most

Compare things using this pattern:
1. **big**
2. **bigger**
3. **biggest**

Tell about people you know who are:
smart
1. _____
2. _____
3.

Find something in the room that is:
1. **small**
2. _____
3. _____

Tell about something that you saw that was:
1. **impressive**
2. _____ _____
3. _____ _____

With 3 or more syllables, use more and most
1. **beautiful**
2. _____ _____
3. _____ _____

Tell about somewhere that you went that was:
1. **far**
2. _____
3. _____

WRITING

Describe

FILL IN THE BLANKS

Irregular Verbs & Past Participles

MAIN VERB	PAST	PRESENT	FUTURE	Have Has Had	PAST PARTICIPLE
damage			will / going to	Have Has Had	
dance			will / going to	Have Has Had	
decide			will / going to	Have Has Had	
decorate			will / going to	Have Has Had	
decrease			will / going to	Have Has Had	
drink			will / going to	Have Has Had	
dig			will / going to	Have Has Had	
do			will / going to	Have Has Had	
draw			will / going to	Have Has Had	
drive			will / going to	Have Has Had	

I
we
you
they   have

he
she
it   has

I
we
you
they
he
she
it   had

FILL IN THE BLANKS

VERB: DECIDE

	PAST	PRESENT	FUTURE
SIMPLE	+ed, new word, did not, did? (I,we,you,they)(he,she,it) 1. ____ ____ to go. 2. ____ ____ ____ to go. 3. ____ ____ ____ to go?	verb, +s,es, do not, do? (I,we,you,they)(he,she,it) 1. ____ ____ to go. 2. ____ ____ ____ to go. 3. ____ ____ ____ to go?	will, will not, will? (I,we,you,they)(he,she,it) 1. ____ ____ to go. 2. ____ ____ ____ to go. 3. ____ ____ ____ to go?
CONTINUOUS +ing = action continues for a time	was, were, +ing, not, ? (we,you,they)(I,he,she,it) 1. ____ ____ ____ to go. 2. ____ ____ ____ to go. 3. ____ ____ ____ to gor?	am, is, are, not, ? (I)(we,you,they)(he,she,it) 1. ____ ____ ____ to go. 2. ____ ____ ____ to go. 3. ____ ____ ____ to go?	will be, will not be, will ? (we,you,they)(I,he,she,it) 1. ____ ____ ____ to go. 2. ____ ____ ____ to go. 3. ____ ____ ____ to go?
PERFECT had, have, has, will have PP actions completed in past, but relates to another time	had, had PP, not PP, had PP? (we,you,they)(I,he,she,it) 1. ____ ____ ____ to go 2. ____ ____ ____ to go. 3. ____ ____ ____ to go?	have, has PP, not PP, PP? (I,we,you,they)(he,she,it) 1. ____ ____ ____ to go. 2. ____ ____ ____ to go. 3. ____ ____ ____ to go?	will have PP, will not have PP, PP? (I,we,you,they)(he,she,it) 1. ____ ____ ____ to go. 2. ____ ____ ____ to go. 3. ____ ____ ____ to go?
PERFECT CONTINUOUS +had,have,has been completed, but will continue	had been +ing, had not been +ing, Had __ +ing? (we,you,they)(I,he,she,it) 1. ____ ____ ____ to go. 2. ____ ____ ____ to go. 3. ____ ____ ____ to go?	have, has been +ing, not been +ing, been +ing? (I,we,you,they)(he,she,it) 1. ____ ____ ____ to go. 2. ____ ____ ____ to go. 3. ____ ____ ____ to go?	will have been +ing, will not, +ing? (I,we,you,they)(he,she,it) 1. ____ ____ ____ to go. 2. ____ ____ ____ to go. 3. ____ ____ ____ to go?

EXTRA HOMEWORK: Watch the movie *Facing the Giants.* Set the subtitles to your language so you can understand the story. Answer these questions.

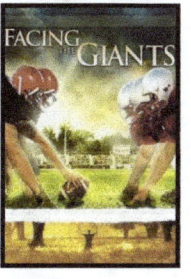

Movie Review Questions:

1. What was your favorite part of the movie?
2. What did Coach Grant do to change his football team?
3. At practice, what did Coach Grant teach the team captain, Brock, about not giving up?
4. What do you think it means to praise God when we win and also when we lose?
5. What other ways did God bless Coach Grant other than winning football games?

Lesson 5 — Saul to Paul

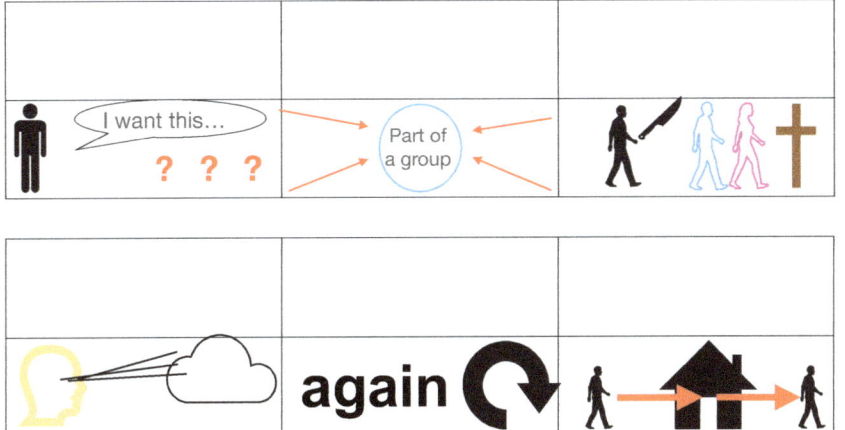

REVIEW WHAT YOU KNOW:

The opposite of come is _____	
Write the contraction for "He would."	
How many states are in the United States?	
Write the name of the fourth month.	

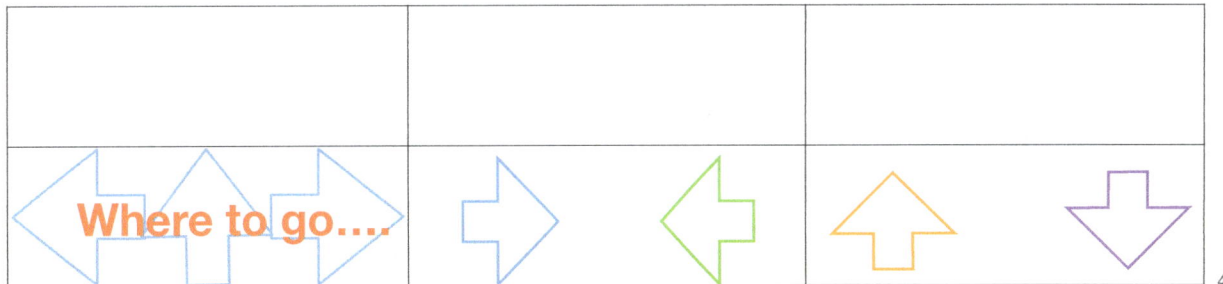

VOCABULARY

Abstract Things

Some things are things that we cannot see.
Name as many as you can in each category.

Feelings	Go on a...	Qualities... we have...	Ideals, Concepts, Beliefs	More

`BIBLE` # Acts 9

The Bible says:
9:1 "Meanwhile, Saul was still breathing threats and murder against the disciples of the Lord. He went to the high priest
9:2 and requested letters from him to the synagogues in Damascus, so that if he found any men or women who belonged to the Way, he might bring them as prisoners to Jerusalem.
9:3 As he traveled and was nearing Damascus, a light from heaven suddenly flashed around him.
9:4 Falling to the ground, he heard a voice saying to him, 'Saul, Saul, why are you persecuting Me?'
9:5 'Who are You, Lord?' he said. 'I am Jesus, the One you are persecuting,' He replied.
9:6 'But get up and go into the city, and you will be told what you must do.'
9:7 The men who were traveling with him stood speechless, hearing the sound but seeing no one.
9:8 Then Saul got up from the ground, and though his eyes were open, he could see nothing. So they took him by the hand and let him into Damascus.
9:9 He was unable to see for three days and did not eat or drink." Acts 9:1-9 HCSB

In your own words:
9:1-2 Saul was trying to stop the people who believed in Jesus, so he _____
_____.
9:2 The followers of Jesus were sometimes called "The Way" because Jesus said in John 14:6, "I am _____
_____.
9:4 Jesus asked Saul, _____.
9:5 Jesus said that Saul was persecuting Him because _____.
9:9 Saul went to the city and _____.

BIBLE   # Acts 9

The Bible says,

9:10 "There was a disciple in Damascus named Ananias, And the Lord said to him in a vision, 'Ananias!' 'Here I am, Lord!' he said.

9:11 'Get up and go to the street called Straight.' the Lord said to him, 'to the house of Judas, and ask for a man from Tarsus named Saul, since he is praying there.

9:12 In a vision he has seen a man named Ananias coming in and placing his hands on him so he can regain his sight.'

9:13 'Lord,' Ananias answered, 'I have heard from many people about this man, how much harm he has done to Your saints in Jerusalem.

9:14 And he has authority here from the chief priests to arrest all who call on Your name.'

9:15 But the Lord said to him, 'Go! For this is My chosen instrument to take My name to Gentiles, kings, and the Israelites.

9:16 I will show him how much he must suffer for My name!'" Acts 9:10-16 HCSB

In your own words:

9:13 Ananias seemed a little scared to go see Saul because _____.

9:15 God chose Saul even though _____.

 # Acts 9

The Bible says,
9:17 "So Ananias left and entered the house. Then he placed his hands on him and said, 'Brother Saul, the Lord Jesus, who appeared to you on the road you were traveling has sent me so that you can regain your sight and be filled with the Holy Spirit.'
9:18 At once something like scales fell from his eyes, and he regained his sight. Then he got up and was baptized.
9:19 And after taking some food, he regained his strength. Saul was with the disciples in Damascus for some days.
9:20 Immediately he began proclaiming Jesus in the synagogues; 'He is the Son of God.'
9:21 But all who heard him were astounded and said, 'Isn't this the man who, in Jerusalem, was destroying those who called on this name and then came here for the purpose of taking them as prisoners to the chief priests?'
9:26 When he arrived in Jerusalem, he tried to associate with the disciples, but they were all afraid of him since they did not believe he was a disciple.
9:27 Barnabas, however, took him and brought him to the apostles and explained to them how Saul had seen the Lord on the road and that He had talked to him, and how in Damascus he had spoken boldly in the name of Jesus.
9:28 Saul was coming and going with them in Jerusalem, speaking boldly in the name of the Lord." Acts 9 HCSB

In your own words:
9:17 Ananias knew Saul was now a part of God's spiritual family, so he called him,_____.

LET'S TALK

Directions
Look at the map and answer these questions:

1. What is between the bank and the park?

   _____

2. How do I get from the police station to the school?

   _____

3. What is near the clothing store?

   _____

4. Is the stadium close to the church?

   _____

5. Where is the neighborhood?

   _____

6. Where is the business district?

   _____

7. How do I get from the hospital to the stadium?

   _____

8. How many hotels are in the city?

   _____

9. How many factories are in the city?

   _____

10. What is across the street from the farm?

   _____

LET'S TALK Directions

WRITING

Describe

56

FILL IN THE BLANKS — Irregular Verbs & Past Participles

MAIN VERB	← PAST	↓ PRESENT	→ FUTURE	Have/Has/Had	PAST PARTICIPLE
earn			will / going to	Have/Has/Had	
eat			will / going to	Have/Has/Had	
empty			will / going to	Have/Has/Had	
encourage			will / going to	Have/Has/Had	
enjoy			will / going to	Have/Has/Had	
erase			will / going to	Have/Has/Had	
fall			will / going to	Have/Has/Had	
feel			will / going to	Have/Has/Had	
fight			will / going to	Have/Has/Had	
forget			will / going to	Have/Has/Had	

I / we / you / they — have
he / she / it — has
I / we / you / they / he / she / it — had

FILL IN THE BLANKS

VERB: ENJOY

	PAST	PRESENT	FUTURE
SIMPLE	+ed, new word, did not, did? (I,we,you,they)(he,she,it) 1. ____ _____ soccer. 2. ___ _____ ___ _____ soccer. 3. ___ ___ _____ soccer?	verb, +s,es, do not, do? (I,we,you,they)(he,she,it) 1. ____ _____ soccer. 2. _____ _____ ___ _____ soccer 3. ___ _____ _____ soccer?	will, will not, will? (I,we,you,they)(he,she,it) 1. _____ _____ _____ soccer. 2. _____ _____ _____ soccer. 3. _____ _____ _____ soccer?
CONTINUOUS +ing = action continues for a time	was, were, +ing, not, ? (we,you,they)(I,he,she,it) 1. _____ _____ _____ soccer. 2. _____ _____ _____ soccer. 3. _____ _____ _____ soccer?	am,is,are, not, ? (I)(we,you,they)(he,she,it) 1. _____ _____ _____ soccer. 2. _____ _____ ___ _____ soccer. 3. _____ _____ _____ soccer?	will be, will not be, will ? (we,you,they)(I,he,she,it) 1. _____ _____ _____ soccer. 2. _____ _____ _____ soccer. 3. ___ ___ _____ soccer?
PERFECT had,have,has,will have PP actions completed in past, but relates to another time	had, had PP, not PP, had PP? (we,you,they)(I,he,she,it) 1. ____ _____ _____ soccer. 2. _____ _____ ___ _____ soccer. 3. ___ _____ _____ soccer?	have, has PP, not PP, PP? (I,we,you,they)(he,she,it) 1. _____ _____ _____ soccer. 2. _____ _____ ___ _____ soccer. 3. _____ _____ _____ soccer?	will have PP, will not have PP, PP? (I,we,you,they)(he,she,it) 1. _____ _____ _____ soccer. 2. _____ _____ ___ _____ soccer. 3. _____ _____ _____ soccer?
PERFECT CONTINUOUS +had,have,has been completed, but will continue	had been +ing, had not been +ing, Had __ +ing? (we,you,they)(I,he,she,it) 1. ____ _____ _____ soccer. 2. _____ _____ _____ soccer. 3. ___ _____ _____ soccer?	have, has been +ing, not been +ing, been +ing? (I,we,you,they)(he,she,it) 1. _____ _____ _____ soccer. 2. ___ ___ _____ soccer. 3. ___ ___ soccer?	will have been +ing, will not, +ing? (I,we,you,they)(he,she,it) 1. ____ _____ _____ soccer. 2. ___ _____ _____ soccer. 3. _____ _____ _____ soccer?

EXTRA

EXTRA HOMEWORK: Watch the movie *War Room.* Set the subtitles to your language so you can understand the story. Answer these questions.

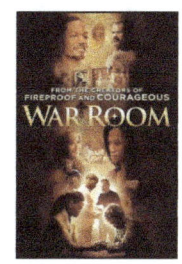

Movie Review Questions:

1. What was your favorite part of the movie?
2. What happened on Tony's business trip when Elizabeth started praying for him?
3. What sport does Danielle like to do?
4. How would you describe Miss Clara?
5. Why does Miss Clara call her prayer room a war room?

VOCABULARY

Lesson 6

Answered Prayer

I like this. ✓ I am happy.	I will…. I plan to…..	

I know who you are.	😲😮	

REVIEW WHAT YOU KNOW:

What is the first day of the week?	
Write 57 times 2 equals…	
Draw something you see in the summer.	
We drive our cars on the _____.	

Funny phrases that have different meanings		

Adverbs

Adverbs describe how we do things.
Name as many as you can in each category.

How we live	How we eat	How we learn	How we work	How we love

| BIBLE | Acts 12 |

The Bible says,

12:1"About that time King Herod cruelly attacked some who belonged to the church,

12:2 and he killed James, John's brother, with the sword.

12:3 When he saw that it pleased the Jews, he proceeded to arrest Peter too, during the days of Unleavened Bread.

12:4 After the arrest, he put him in prison and assigned four squads of four soldiers each to guard him, intending to bring him out to the people after the Passover.

12:5 So Peter was kept in prison, but prayer was being made earnestly to God for him by the church.

12:6 On the night before Herod was to bring him out for execution, Peter, bound with two chains, was sleeping between two soldiers, while the sentries (soldiers) in front of the door guarded the prison.

12:7 Suddenly an angel of the Lord appeared, and a light shone in the cell. Striking Peter on the side, he woke him up and said, 'Quick, get up!' Then the chains fell off his wrists." Acts 121-7 HCSB

In your own words:

12:2 King Herod kept attacking those who believed in Jesus. He even killed _____.

12:5 Herod assigned a lot of guards to Peter, but the church was _____.

12:7 The night before Peter's execution, God _____.

> **BIBLE**

Acts 12

The Bible says,
12:8 "'Get dressed,' the angel told him, 'and put on your sandals,' And he did so. 'Wrap your cloak around you,' he told him, 'and follow me.'
12:9 So he went out and followed, and he did not know that what took place through the angel was real, but thought he was seeing a vision.
12:10 After they passed the first and second guard posts, they came to the iron gate that leads into the city, which opened to them by itself. They went outside and passed one street, and immediately the angel left him.
12:11 Then Peter came to himself and said, 'Now I know for certain that the Lord has sent His angel and rescued me from Herod's grasp and from all that the Jewish people expected.'" Acts 12:8-11HCSB

In your own words:
12:9 Since Peter had been asleep he wasn't sure if _____.
12:10 The large iron gate to the city _____.
12:11 Peter then realized that _____.

| BIBLE | Acts 12 |

The Bible says,
12:12 "When he realized this, he went to the house of Mary, the mother of John Mark, where many had assembled and were praying.
12:13 He knocked at the door in the gateway, and a servant named Rhoda came to answer.
12:14 She recognized Peter's voice, and because of her joy, she did not open the gate but ran in and announced that Peter was standing at the gateway.
12:15 'You're crazy!' they told her. But she kept insisting that is was true. Then they said, 'It's his angel!'
12:16 Peter, however kept on knocking, and when they opened the door and saw him, they were astounded.
12:17 Motioning to them with his hand to be silent, he explained to them how the Lord had brought him out of the prison. 'Report these things to James and the brothers,' he said. Then he departed and went to a different place." Acts 12:12-17HCSB

In your own words:
12:15 The people had been praying that God would get Peter out of prison, but when Peter showed up at the house, _____.
12:17 Peter told them the story and then he told them to _____.

Application:
- Sometimes God rescues His followers by bringing them on to Heaven, but sometimes He sends an angel or someone to rescue. Do you ever think of death as being rescued or healed?
- Do you think you could sleep like Peter did the night before your execution?
- Do you pray expecting God to answer, or are you surprised when He does?

LET'S TALK

Idioms

24 / 7		👂👂👂👂	
🫃		🖼️ = 1,000 words	
🐟 〰️		🏵️	
🦶 👄		📖	
☁️		💵 → 🧍	
🪡 🌾		☁️ 9	
🐈‍⬛ 🛍️		1 🌙	

WRITING

Describe

FILL IN THE BLANKS — **Irregular Verbs & Past Participles**

MAIN VERB	← PAST	↓ PRESENT	→ FUTURE	Have/Has/Had	PAST PARTICIPLE
get			will / going to	Have/Has/Had	
give			will / going to	Have/Has/Had	
grow			will / going to	Have/Has/Had	
go			will / going to	Have/Has/Had	
hang			will / going to	Have/Has/Had	
have			will / going to	Have/Has/Had	
hit			will / going to	Have/Has/Had	
hug			will / going to	Have/Has/Had	
hurt			will / going to	Have/Has/Had	
heal			will / going to	Have/Has/Had	

I / we / you / they — have
he / she / it — has
I / we / you / they / he / she / it — had

FILL IN THE BLANKS

VERB: GO

	PAST	PRESENT	FUTURE
SIMPLE	+ed,new word, did not, did? (I,we,you,they)(he,she,it) 1. ____ _____ home. 2. ___ ____ ___ _____ home. 3. ___ ____ _____ home?	verb, +s,es,do not, do? (I,we,you,they)(he,she,it) 1. ____ _____ home. 2._____ ____ ___ _____ home. 3. ___ _____ _____ home?	will, will not, will? (I,we,you,they)(he,she,it) 1. _____ _____ home. 2. ____ ____ ___ _____ home. 3. ___ _____ _____ home?
CONTINUOUS +ing = action continues for a time	was, were, +ing, not, ? (we,you,they)(I,he,she,it) 1. _____ _____ home. 2. _____ ____ ___ _____ home. 3. _____ ____ _____ home?	am,is,are, not, ? (I)(we,you,they)(he,she,it) 1. _____ _____ home. 2. _____ ____ ___ _____ home. 3. _____ _____ _____ home	will be, will not be, will ? (we,you,they)(I,he,she,it) 1. _____ _____ home. 2._____ ____ ___ _____ home. 3. ___ _____ _____ home?
PERFECT had,have,has,will have PP actions completed in past, but relates to another time	had, had PP, not PP, had PP? (we,you,they)(I,he,she,it) 1.____ ____ _____ home. 2._____ ___ ___ _____ home. 3. ___ _____ _____ home?	have, has PP, not PP, PP? (I,we,you,they)(he,she,it) 1._____ ___ _____ home. 2._____ ____ ___ _____ home. 3. ___ _____ _____ home?	will have PP, will not have PP, PP? (I,we,you,they)(he,she,it) 1._____ ___ ____ _____ home. 2._____ ____ ___ ___ _____ home. 3. ___ _____ _____ _____ home?
PERFECT CONTINUOUS +had,have,has been completed, but will continue	had been +ing, had not been +ing, Had __ +ing? (we,you,they)(I,he,she,it) 1. _____ ____ ____ _____ home. 2. _____ ___ ___ ___ _____ home. 3. ___ _____ ____ ___ _____ home?	have, has been +ing, not been +ing, been +ing? (I,we,you,they)(he,she,it) 1. _____ ___ ____ ___ ____ home. 2. ____ ___ ___ ___ _____ home. 3. ____ ____ ___ _____ home?	will have been +ing, will not, +ing? (I,we,you,they)(he,she,it) 1. ____ ___ ____ ____ home. 2.____ ___ ___ ___ ____ home. 3. ___ _____ ___ _____ home?

EXTRA HOMEWORK: Watch the movie *Overcomer.* Set the subtitles to your language so you can understand the story. Answer these questions.

Movie Review Questions:

1. What was your favorite part of the movie?
2. What things does Hannah have to overcome in life?
3. Why did Coach Harrison have to start coaching Cross Country?
4. Who is Thomas Hill?
5. How did Thomas Hill help Hannah in the last race?

VOCABULARY **Lesson 7** **Sorcery and Assistants**

helping serving giving		

		not good enough do not deserve

REVIEW WHAT YOU KNOW:

Write the homophones for	
What is the seventh month?	
What do you need to unlock your house?	
Where do we go to eat out?	

Prepositions

Prepositions are words that go with nouns or pronouns and tell how they relate to another word. They are used in phrases. We can usually think of them in relation to a chair. Something can be … the chair.

With a and b	With c, d, e and f	With i, l, n and o	With p, t and u	With w

`BIBLE`

Acts 13

The Bible says,
13:2 "As they were ministering to the Lord and fasting, the Holy Spirit (God) said, 'Set apart for Me Barnabas and Saul for the work I have called them to.'
13:3 Then after they had fasted, prayed, and laid hands on them, they sent them off.
13:4 Being sent out by the Holy Spirit (God), they came down to Seleucia, and from there they sailed to Cyprus.
13:5 Arriving in Salamis, they proclaimed God's message in the Jewish synagogues. They also had John (John Mark) as their assistant.
13:6 When they had gone through the whole island as far as Paphos, they came across a sorcerer, a Jewish false prophet name Bar-Jesus.
13:7 He was with the proconsul, Sergius Paulus, and intelligent man. This man summoned Barnabus and Saul and desired to hear God's message.
13:8 But Leymas the sorcerer (this is the meaning of his name) opposed them and tried to turn the proconsul away from the faith." Acts 13:2-8HCSB

In your own words:
13:2 This was the first missionary (someone sent out) journey. The church knew who to send because

_____

_____.
13:3 To send them off, the leaders in the church _____.
13:6 One of the first people that they meet when they went out to tell the good news about Jesus was a

_____.

BIBLE
Acts 13

The Bible says,
13:9 "Then Saul - also called Paul - filled with the Holy Spirit (God), stared straight at the sorcerer
13:10 and said, 'You son of the Devil, full of all deceit and all fraud, enemy of all righteousness! Won't you ever stop perverting the straight paths of the Lord?
13:11 Now, look! The Lord's hand is against you. You are going to be blind, and will not see the sun for a time.' Suddenly a mist and darkness fell on him, and he went around seeking someone to lead him by the hand.
13:12 Then the proconsul, seeing what happened, believed and was astonished at the teaching about the Lord." Acts 13:9-12HCSB

In your own words:
13:9 Saul got a new name when he began his new spiritual life of following Jesus. Now his name is _____.
13:10 Paul called out the sorcerer. He said he was _____.
13:11 Paul told him that he would be _____.
13:12 The proconsul (The Roman leader of an area) believed when _____.

| BIBLE | Acts 13 |

The Bible says,
13:44 "The following Sabbath almost the whole town assembled to hear the message of the Lord.
13:45 But then the Jews saw the crowds, they were filled with jealousy and began to oppose what Paul was saying by insulting him.
13:46 Then Paul and Barnabas boldly said: 'It was necessary that God's message be spoken to you first. But since you reject it and consider yourselves unworthy of eternal life, we now turn to the Gentiles (everyone who is not a Jew)!
13:47 For this is what the Lord has commanded us: 'I have made you a light for the Gentiles to bring salvation to the ends of the earth."
13:48 When the Gentiles heard this, they rejoiced and glorified the message of the Lord, and all who had been appointed to eternal life believed.
13:49 So the message of the Lord spread through the whole region." Acts 13:44-49HCSB

In your own words:
13:45 Some of the Jews thought that they were the only ones that could be saved so they _____
13:46 The Jews were told about salvation from Jesus first, and then _____
13:48 The Gentiles were very happy and many of them _____.

Application:
- Have you ever had a desire to go to a new place and tell people about Jesus and the new life and Heaven that is only from Him?

LET'S TALK

Idioms

WRITING

Describe

FILL IN THE BLANKS

Irregular Verbs & Past Participles

MAIN VERB	← PAST	↓ PRESENT	→ FUTURE	Have / Has / Had	PAST PARTICIPLE
identify			will / going to	Have/Has/Had	
imitate			will / going to	Have/Has/Had	
impress			will / going to	Have/Has/Had	
include			will / going to	Have/Has/Had	
inform			will / going to	Have/Has/Had	
inherit			will / going to	Have/Has/Had	
inspect			will / going to	Have/Has/Had	
inspire			will / going to	Have/Has/Had	
jump			will / going to	Have/Has/Had	
justify			will / going to	Have/Has/Had	

I / we / you / they — have
he / she / it — has
I / we / you / they / he / she / it — had

FILL IN THE BLANKS

VERB: INSPECT

	PAST	PRESENT	FUTURE
SIMPLE	+ed,new word, did not, did? (I,we,you,they)(he,she,it) 1. _____ _____ the car. 2. ___ _____ ___ _____ the car. 3. ___ ____ _____ the car.	verb, +s,es,do not, do? (I,we,you,they)(he,she,it) 1. ____ _____ the car.. 2.____ _____ ___ _____ the car. 3. _____ _____ _____ the car.?	will, will not, will? (I,we,you,they)(he,she,it) 1. _____ _____ the car. 2. _____ _____ ___ _____ the car. 3. _____ _____ _____ the car?
CONTINUOUS +ing = action continues for a time	was, were, +ing, not, ? (we,you,they)(I,he,she,it) 1. _____ _____ _____ the car. 2. ____ _____ _____ the car. 3. _____ _____ _____ the car?	am,is,are, not, ? (I)(we,you,they)(he,she,it) 1. _____ _____ _____ the car.. 2. ____ _____ ___ _____ the car.. 3. _____ _____ _____ the car.?	will be, will not be, will ? (we,you,they)(I,he,she,it) 1. _____ _____ _____ the car. 2._____ _____ _____ the car. 3. ___ ____ _____ the car?
PERFECT had,have,has will have PP actions completed in past, but relates to another time	had, had PP, not PP, had PP? (we,you,they)(I,he,she,it) 1.____ ____ _____ the car. 2._____ ____ ___ _____ the car. 3. ___ _____ _____ the car?	have, has PP, not PP, PP? (I,we,you,they)(he,she,it) 1. _____ _____ _____ the car. 2. _____ _____ ___ _____ the car. 3. _____ _____ _____ the car?	will have PP, will not have PP, PP? (I,we,you,they)(he,she,it) 1._____ _____ _____ the car. 2. _____ _____ ___ _____ the car. 3. _____ _____ _____ the car.?
PERFECT CONTINUOUS +had,have,has been completed, but will continue	had been +ing, had not been +ing, Had __ +ing? (we,you,they)(I,he,she,it) 1. ____ _____ _____ the car. 2. _____ _____ _____ the car 3. _____ _____ _____ the car.?	have, has been +ing, not been +ing, been +ing? (I,we,you,they)(he,she,it) 1. _____ _____ _____ the car. 2. ____ _____ ___ _____ the car. 3. ____ _____ _____ the car?	will have been +ing, will not, +ing? (I,we,you,they)(he,she,it) 1. ____ _____ _____ the car.. 2.____ _____ _____ the car. 3. ___ _____ _____ the car.?

EXTRA HOMEWORK: Watch the movie *Flywheel*. Set the subtitles to your language so you can understand the story. Answer these questions.

Movie Review Questions:

1. What was your favorite part of the movie?
2. What did Jay do that was not right?
3. What happened that made Jay want to change?
4. What did Jay do to make things right?
5. What was a funny part of the movie?

 **VOCABULARY**

Lesson 8

Earthquake

	😠	
		hurt places on a body

REVIEW WHAT YOU KNOW:

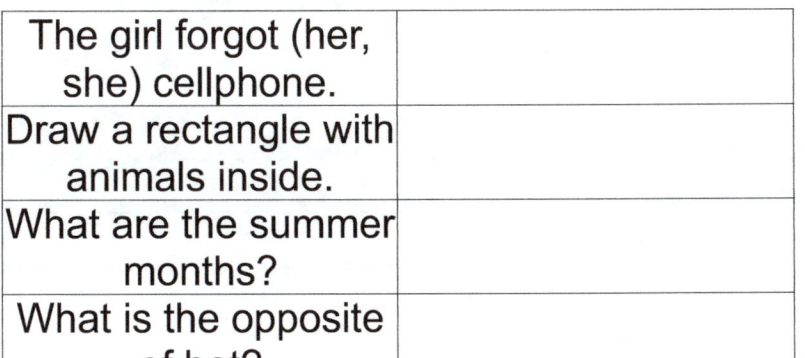

The girl forgot (her, she) cellphone.	
Draw a rectangle with animals inside.	
What are the summer months?	
What is the opposite of hot?	

groups, sections	**hear / listen**	

Things you like to....

Improve you vocabulary by listing things that you like to do, and add things that you didn't think of at first.

eat...	do at work...	do with your free time...	buy...	watch on TV

| BIBLE | <div align="center"># Acts 16</div> |

The Bible says,

16:1 "Then he (Paul) went on to Derbe and Lystra, where there was a disciple named Timothy, the son of a believing Jewish woman, but his father was a Greek.

16:2 The brothers in Lystra and Iconium spoke highly of him.

16:3 Paul wanted Timothy to go with him…

16:12 "and from there (the port city) to Philippi, a Roman colony, which is a leading city of that district of Macedonia. We stayed in that city for a number of days.

16:13 On the Sabbath day we went outside the city gate by the river, where we thought there was a place of prayer. We sat down and spoke to the women gathered there.

16:14 A woman named Lydia, a dealer in purple cloth from the city of Thyatira, who worshiped God, was listening. The Lord opened her heart to pay attention to what was spoken by Paul.

16:15 After she and her household were baptized, she urged us, 'If you consider me a believer in the Lord, come and stay at my house.' And she persuaded us." Acts 16:1-3,12-15HCSB

In your own words:

16:1-2 Timothy became one of the missionaries who traveled with Paul. Paul probably chose him because _____. Later Paul wrote letters to Timothy.

16:12 After the missionaries left the port city, they went to _____. Years later, Paul would write a letter to the believers in this area encouraging them to keep following God. The letter is in the Bible called Philippians.

16:14 Lydia was a _____. God opened her heart to _____

16:15 To show that she and her family believed and followed Jesus they were _____

`BIBLE`   # Acts 16

The Bible says,
16:16 "Once, as we were on our way to prayer, a slave girl met us who had a spirit of prediction (told the future by demons). She made a large profit for her owners by fortune-telling.
16:17 As she followed Paul and us she cried out, 'These men, who are proclaiming to you the way of salvation, are the slaves of the Most High God.'
16:18 And she did this for many days. But Paul was greatly aggravated and turning to the spirit(demon), said, 'I command you in the name of Jesus Christ to come out of her!' And it came out right away.
16:19 When her owners saw that their hope of profit was gone, they seized Paul and Silas and dragged them into the marketplace to the authorities.
16:23 After they had inflicted many blows on them, they threw them in jail, ordering the jailer to keep them securely guarded.
16:24 Receiving such an order, he put them into the inner prison and secured their feet in the stocks."
Acts 16:16-19,23-24HCSB

In your own words:
16:16 The slave girl made money for her owners by _____.
16:18 Paul commanded the spirit (demon) to come of her by the name of _____
16:19 The owners took Paul and Silas to the authorities because _____.
16:24 The missionaries were _____.

BIBLE

Acts 16

The Bible says,

16:25 "About midnight Paul and Silas were praying and singing hymns to God, and the prisoners were listening to them.

16:26 Suddenly there was such a violent earthquake that the foundations of the jail were shaken, and immediately all the doors were opened, and everyone's chains came loose.

16:27 When the jailer woke up and saw the doors of the prison open, he drew his sword and was going to kill himself, since he thought the prisoners had escaped.

16:28 But Paul called out in a loud voice, 'Don't harm yourself, because all of us are here!'

16:29 Then the jailer called for lights, rushed in, and fell down trembling before Paul and Silas.

16:30 Then he escorted them out and said, 'Sirs, what must I do to be saved?'

16:31 So they said, 'Believe on the Lord Jesus, and you will be saved - you and your household.'

16:32 Then they spoke the message of the Lord to him along with everyone in his house.

16:33 He took them the same hour of the night and washed their wounds. Right away he and all his family were baptized.

16:34 He brought them into his house, set a meal before them, and rejoiced because he had believed God with his entire household." Acts 16:25-33HCSB

In your own words:

16:25 Paul and Silas had just been beaten and they were chained in jail, but they were_____

16:26 The earthquake made the _____.

16:28 Not only did Paul and Silas stay after the earthquake, but so did _____.

16:34 The whole family believed in Jesus. They were so happy that they _____

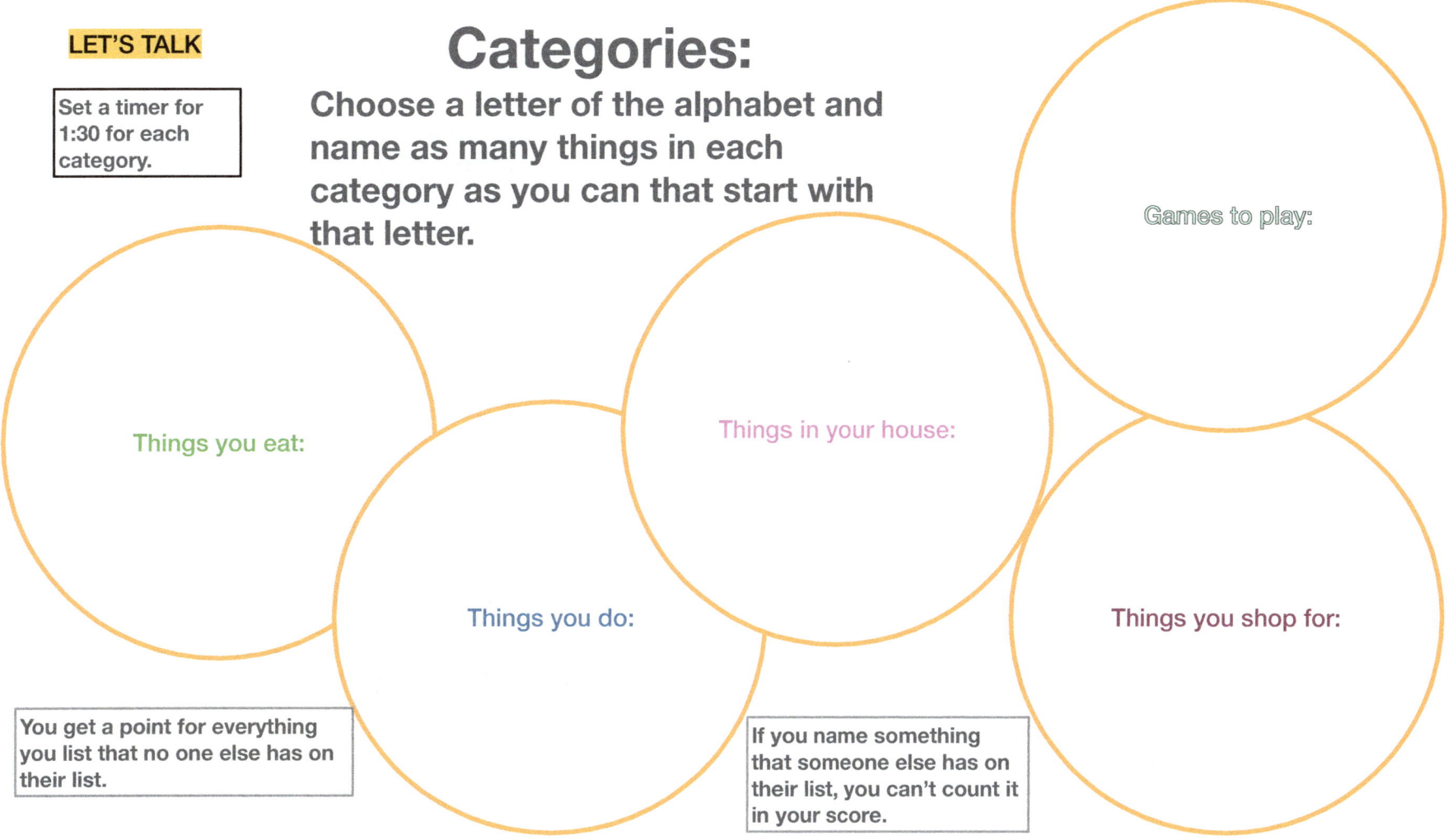

Describe

WRITING

FILL IN THE BLANKS — **Irregular Verbs & Past Participles**

MAIN VERB	← PAST	↓ PRESENT	→ FUTURE	Have/Has/Had	PAST PARTICIPLE
keep			will / going to	Have/Has/Had	
kneel			will / going to	Have/Has/Had	
know			will / going to	Have/Has/Had	
kiss			will / going to	Have/Has/Had	
knock			will / going to	Have/Has/Had	
lay			will / going to	Have/Has/Had	
lead			will / going to	Have/Has/Had	
leave			will / going to	Have/Has/Had	
lie			will / going to	Have/Has/Had	
lift			will / going to	Have/Has/Had	

I / we / you / they — have
he / she / it — has

I / we / you / they — had
he / she / it — had

FILL IN THE BLANKS

VERB: LISTEN

	PAST	PRESENT	FUTURE
SIMPLE	+ed, new word, did not, did? (I,we,you,they)(he,she,it) 1. _____ _____ to music. 2. ___ _____ __ _____ to music. 3. ___ ____ _____ to music. ?	verb, +s,es,do not, do? (I,we,you,they)(he,she,it) 1. ____ _____ to music. 2.____ _____ ___ _____ to music. 3. ___ _____ _____ to music?	will, will not, will? (I,we,you,they)(he,she,it) 1. _____ _____ to music. 2. ____ ____ ___ ____ to music. 3. ___ _____ ___ to music?
CONTINUOUS +ing = action continues for a time	was, were, +ing, not, ? (we,you,they)(I,he,she,it) 1. _____ _____ _____ to music. 2. ____ _____ ____ _____ to music. 3. _____ _____ _____ to music?	am,is,are, not, ? (I)(we,you,they)(he,she,it) 1. _____ _____ _____ to music. 2. ____ _____ __ _____ to music. 3. _____ _____ _____ to music?	will be, will not be, will ? (we,you,they)(I,he,she,it) 1. _____ _____ _____ to music. 2.____ _____ ___ _____ to music. 3. ____ ___ _____ to music?
PERFECT had,have,has,will have PP actions completed in past, but relates to another time	had, had PP, not PP, had PP? (we,you,they)(I,he,she,it) 1.____ _____ to music. 2._____ ____ __ _____ to music. 3. ___ _____ _____ to music?	have, has PP, not PP, PP? (I,we,you,they)(he,she,it) 1. _____ _____ _____ to music. 2._____ _____ ___ _____ to music. 3. _____ _____ _____ to music?	will have PP, will not have PP, PP? (I,we,you,they)(he,she,it) 1._____ _____ _____ _____ to music. 2. ____ ____ ____ ____ _____ to music. 3. _____ _____ _____ _____ to music?
PERFECT CONTINUOUS +had,have,has been completed, but will continue	had been +ing, had not been +ing, Had __ +ing? (we,you,they)(I,he,she,it) 1. _____ _____ _____ _____ to music. 2. _____ __ ____ _____ _____ to music. 3. ____ _____ ____ _____ to music?	have, has been +ing, not been +ing, been +ing? (I,we,you,they)(he,she,it) 1. _____ _____ _____ _____ to music. 2. ____ ____ __ ____ _____ to music. 3. ____ _____ ___ _____ to music?	will have been +ing, will not, +ing? (I,we,you,they)(he,she,it) 1. ____ _____ _____ _____ to music. 2.____ _____ ____ ____ to music. 3. _____ _____ _____ to music?

EXTRA HOMEWORK: Watch the movie *Risen*. Set the subtitles to your language so you can understand the story.

Movie Review Questions:

Write your own questions that you can ask the other students in class to see what they remember from the movie.
Question One:
Question Two:
Question Three:

VOCABULARY

Lesson 9

Explaining the Bible

REVIEW WHAT YOU KNOW:

discuss help understand		
	something made by people that they worship as god	

Contractions for "is not" "I will" "there is"	
five thousand divided by five hundred equals	
How many students are in your class?	
Draw something that you see in the sky.	

What order?	added **before** a word added **after** a word	**To do the wrong way**

Things you don't like to....

Improve you vocabulary by listing things that you don't like to do, and add things that you didn't think of at first.

eat...	do at work...	clean...	say...	watch on TV

| BIBLE |

Acts 17

The Bible says,
17:1 "Then they traveled through Amphipolis and Apollonia and came to Thessalonica, where there was a Jewish synagogue.
17:2 As usual, Paul went to the synagogue, and on three Sabbath days reasoned with them from the Scriptures,
17:3 explaining and showing that the Messiah had to suffer and rise from the dead: 'This Jesus I am proclaiming to you is the Messiah.'
17:4 Then some of them were persuaded and joined Paul and Silas including a great number of God-fearing Greeks, as well as a number of the leading women.
17:5 But the Jews became jealous, and they brought together some scoundrels from the marketplace, formed a mob, and started a riot in the city. Attacking Jason's house, they searched for them to bring them out to the public assembly." Acts 17:1-5HCSB

In your own words:
17:1-2 Paul traveled through many cities with several other believers and missionaries. Chapter 17 begins Paul's second missionary journey where he comes to a city called Thessalonica. Later Paul wrote a letter to the Christians here called Thessalonians. Just like in the other cities, Paul went to the _____.
17:3 Paul had the same message that _____.
17:4-5 Some believed in Jesus and some _____.

BIBLE ## Acts 17

The Bible says,
17:10 "As soon as it was night, the brothers sent Paul and Silas off to Berea. On arrival, they went into the synagogue of the Jews.
17:11 The people here were more open-minded than those in Thessalonica, since they welcomed the message with eagerness and examined the Scriptures daily to see if these things were so.
17:12 Consequently, many of them believed, including a number of the prominent Greek women as well as men.
17:13 But when the Jews from Thessalonica found out that God's message had been proclaimed by Paul at Berea, they came there too, agitating and disturbing the crowds.
17:14 Then the brothers immediately sent Paul away to go to the sea, but Silas and Timothy stayed on there.
17:15 Those who escorted Paul brought him as fas as Athens, and after receiving instructions for Silas and Timothy to come to him as quickly as possible, they departed." Acts 17:10-15HCSB

In your own words:
17:11 The believers in Jesus in Berea tested what they were told by _____
17:13 Many of them _____.
17:14 The people who believed in Jesus knew that they all belonged to God's forever family so they called each other _____

BIBLE	Acts 17

The Bible says,

17:16 "While Paul was waiting for them in Athens, his spirit was troubled with him when he saw that the city was full of idols.

17:22 Then Paul stood in the middle of the Areopagus (court in Athens) and said: 'Men of Athens! I see that you are extremely religious in every respect.

17:23 For as I was passing through and observing the objects of your worship, I even found an altar on which was inscribed: 'TO AN UNKNOWN GOD.' Therefore, what you worship in ignorance, this I proclaim to you.

17:24 The God who made the world and everything in it - He is Lord of heaven and earth and does not live in shrines made by hands.

17:25 Neither is He served by human hands, as though He needed anything, since He Himself gives everyone life and breath and all things.

17:26 From one man He has made every nationality to live over the whole earth and has determined their appointed times and the boundaries of where they live.

17:27 He did this so they might seek God, and perhaps they might reach out and find Him, thought He is not far from each one of us.

17:30 Therefore, having overlooked the times of ignorance, God now commands all people everywhere to repent,

17:31 because He has set a day when He is going to judge the world in righteousness by the Man He has appointed. He has provided proof of this to everyone by raising Him from the dead.'" Acts 17:16,22-27,30-31 HCSB

In your own words:

31 There is only one True God, and one day He will _____.

LET'S TALK

1↓ The green car is ….
2↓ The brown car is ….
3↓ The last car is ….

1→ The yellow car is ….
2→ The pink car is ….
3→ The white car is ….
4→ The sixth car is ….
5→ The red car is ….

ORDINAL NUMBERS

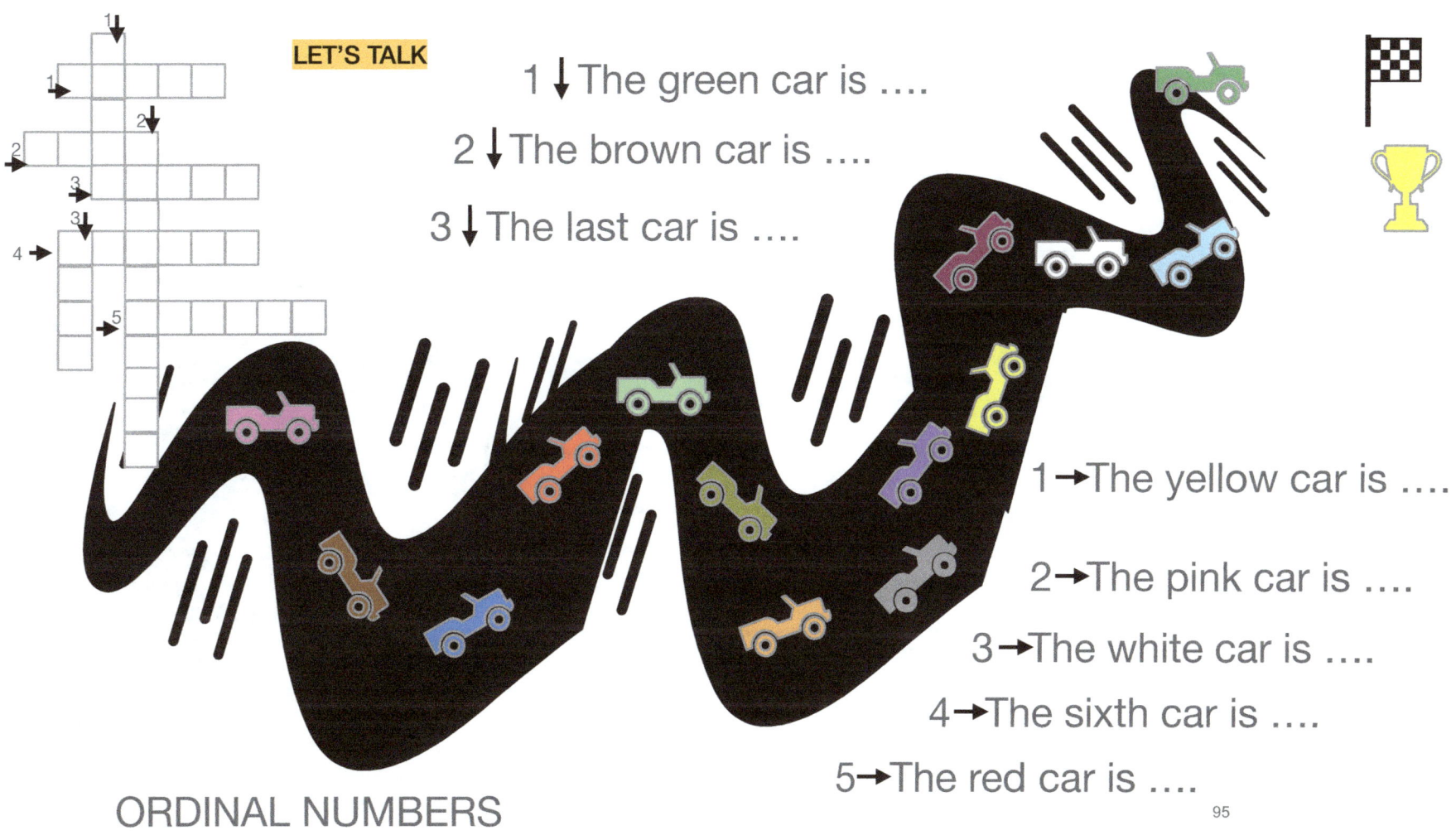

Describe

WRITING

FILL IN THE BLANKS — **Irregular Verbs & Past Participles**

MAIN VERB	← PAST	↓ PRESENT	→ FUTURE	Have/Has/Had	PAST PARTICIPLE
make			will / going to	Have/Has/Had	
meet			will / going to	Have/Has/Had	
mix			will / going to	Have/Has/Had	
move			will / going to	Have/Has/Had	
multiply			will / going to	Have/Has/Had	
notice			will / going to	Have/Has/Had	
need			will / going to	Have/Has/Had	
nap			will / going to	Have/Has/Had	

I / we / you / they — have
he / she / it — has
I / we / you / they / he / she / it — had

FILL IN THE BLANKS

VERB: MOVE

	PAST	PRESENT	FUTURE
SIMPLE	+ed,new word, did not, did? (I,we,you,they)(he,she,it) 1. ____ _____ away. 2. ___ ____ ____ _____ away. 3. ___ ____ ____ away?	verb, +s,es,do not, do? (I,we,you,they)(he,she,it) 1. ____ _____ away. 2. ____ ____ ___ ____ away. 3. ___ _____ away?	will, will not, will? (I,we,you,they)(he,she,it) 1. _____ _____ away. 2. ___ _____ away. 3. ___ _____ away?
CONTINUOUS +ing = action continues for a time	was, were, +ing, not, ? (we,you,they)(I,he,she,it) 1. _____ ____ _____ away. 2. ____ ____ ___ _____ away. 3. _____ ____ away?	am,is,are, not, ? (I)(we,you,they)(he,she,it) 1. _____ ____ ____ away. 2. ____ ____ _____ away. 3. ___ _____ away?	will be, will not be, will ? (we,you,they)(I,he,she,it) 1. ____ ____ _____ away. 2. ___ ____ _____ away. 3. ___ _____ away?
PERFECT had,have,has,will have PP actions completed in past, but relates to another time	had, had PP, not PP, had PP? (we,you,they)(I,he,she,it) 1.____ ___ _____ away. 2._____ ___ ___ _____ away. 3. ___ ____ _____ away?	have, has PP, not PP, PP? (I,we,you,they)(he,she,it) 1. _____ ____ _____ away. 2. _____ ____ _____ away. 3. ___ _____ _____ away?	will have PP, will not have PP, PP? (I,we,you,they)(he,she,it) 1._____ ____ _____ away. 2._____ ____ _____ away. 3. _____ _____ away?
PERFECT CONTINUOUS +had,have,has been completed, but will continue	had been +ing, had not been +ing, Had __ +ing? (we,you,they)(I,he,she,it) 1. _____ _____ _____ away. 2. _____ _____ _____ _____ away. 3. ____ _____ _____ away?	have, has been +ing, not been +ing, been +ing? (I,we,you,they)(he,she,it) 1. _____ _____ _____ away. 2. ____ ____ _____ ____ away. 3. ____ _____ away?	will have been +ing, will not, +ing? (I,we,you,they)(he,she,it) 1. ___ _____ _____ _____ away. 2.____ _____ _____ away. 3. ___ _____ _____ away?

EXTRA

EXTRA HOMEWORK: Watch the movie *Show Me The Father*. Set the subtitles to your language so you can understand the story. Answer these questions.

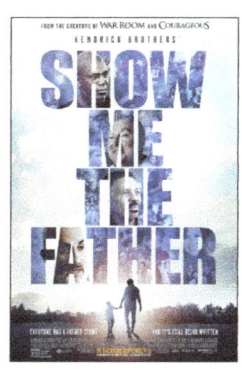

Movie Review Questions:

1. What was your favorite part of the movie?
2. Why did Jim Daly say he needed God to be his Father?
3. What was the big surprise that Deland McCullough found out about his coach?
4. What surprised Stephen Kendrick about his adopted daughter's birthday?
5. How is this movie different from the others that we have watched in this class?

VOCABULARY

Lesson 10

Get Rid of the Evil

		people who God gives the power to cast out demons
		I did it. I was wrong

REVIEW WHAT YOU KNOW:

The girls washed (their, theirs, hers) hands.	
What is the second month of the year?	
We put our shoes on our _____.	
What have you learned in level 4?	

Things that make us better

Physically	Spiritually	Emotionally	Mentally

| BIBLE | Acts 19 |

The Bible says,

19:1 "While Apollos was in Corinth, Paul traveled through the interior regions and came to Ephesus.

19:11 God was performing extraordinary miracles by Paul's hands,

19:12 so that even facecloths or work aprons that had touched his skin were brought to the sick, and the diseases left them, and the evil spirits came out of them." Acts 19:1,11-12 HCSB

In your own words:

19:1 Later Paul wrote letters for the churches in Corinth and Ephesus. These letters were shared with many churches in different areas. They are books of the Bible called 1&2 Corinthians and Ephesians. Apollos stayed in Corinth while Paul _____.

19:11-12 God's power was shown through Paul healing people, but also people were healed by _____.

`BIBLE`   # Acts 19

The Bible says,
19:13 "Then some of the itinerant Jewish exorcists attempted to pronounce the name of the Lord Jesus over those who had evil spirits, saying 'I command you by the Jesus that Paul preaches!'
19:14 Seven sons of Sceva, a Jewish chief priest, were doing this.
19:15 The evil spirit answered them, 'I know Jesus, and I recognize Paul - but who are you?'
19:16 Then the man who had the evil spirit leaped on them, overpowered them all, and prevailed against them, so that they ran out of that house naked and wounded.
19:17 This became known to everyone who lived in Ephesus, both Jews and Greeks. Then fear fell on all of them, and the name of the Lord Jesus was magnified.
19:18 And many who had become believers came confessing and disclosing their practices,
19:19 while many of those who had practiced magic collected their books and burned them in front of everyone. So they calculated their value and found it to be 50,000 pieces of silver.
19:20 In this way the Lord's message flourished and prevailed." Acts 19:13-20 HCSB

In your own words:
19:13-16 The seven sons were trying to use Jesus and Paul's names to cast out demons, but _____ _____.
19:17 This story started making some people _____.
19:18 Many people _____.
19:19 Some who had been using evil and spent money on evil books realized that it didn't matter how much money they lost, they had to _____.

BIBLE

Acts 19

The Bible says,
19:21 "When these events were over, Paul resolved in the Spirit to pass through Macedonia and Achaia and go to Jerusalem….
19:22 So after sending two of those who assisted him, Timothy and Erastus, to Macedonia, he himself stayed in Asia for a while.
19:23 During that time there was a major disturbance about the Way.
19:24 For a person named Demetrius, a silversmith who made silver shrines of Artemis (the idol made by people who believed it controlled fertility), provided a great deal of business for the craftsmen.
19:28 When they had heard this, they were filled with rage and began to cry out, 'Great is Artemis of the Ephesians!'" Acts 19:21-28HCSB

In your own words:
19:23 Jesus said, "I am the way, the truth, and the life. No one comes to the Father except through Me." The people who followed and believed in Him were called _____.
19:24 Demetrius became upset because _____.

Application:
- Have you ever felt like some of the people who heard the story about the demon, where you want to just get rid of anything in your house that might be evil?
- Have you ever had idols? Maybe you didn't worship something that someone made, but maybe you gave more love (time, attention, and money) to something other than God.

Practice using prepositions: above, below, between, beside, beneath, by, in, inside.....

LET'S TALK

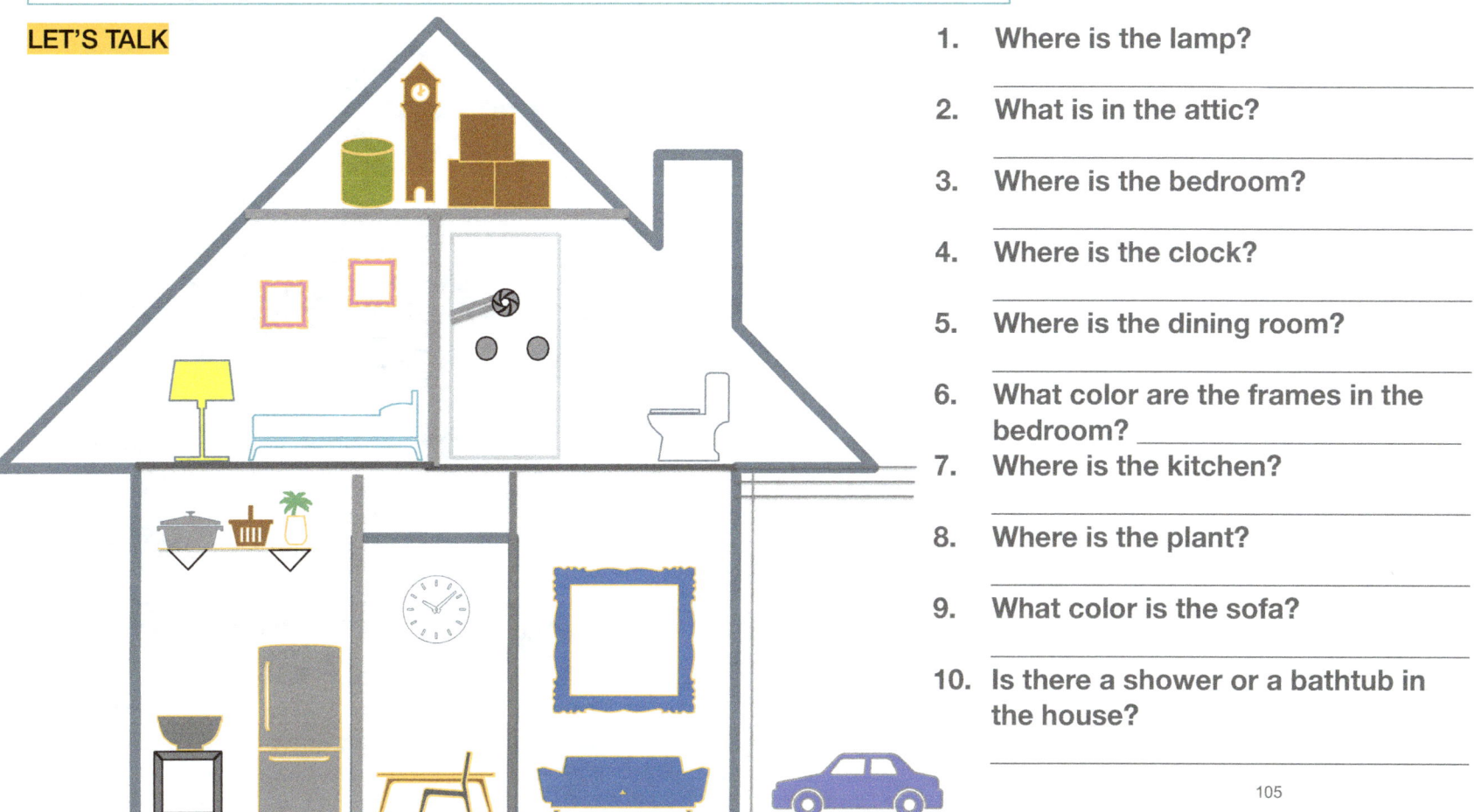

IN THE HOUSE

1. Where is the lamp? _____

2. What is in the attic? _____

3. Where is the bedroom? _____

4. Where is the clock? _____

5. Where is the dining room? _____

6. What color are the frames in the bedroom? _____

7. Where is the kitchen? _____

8. Where is the plant? _____

9. What color is the sofa? _____

10. Is there a shower or a bathtub in the house? _____

105

WRITING

Describe

FILL IN THE BLANKS — **Irregular Verbs & Past Participles**

MAIN VERB	← PAST	↓ PRESENT	→ FUTURE	Have Has Had	PAST PARTICIPLE
obey			will / going to	Have Has Had	
observe			will / going to	Have Has Had	
offer			will / going to	Have Has Had	
owe			will / going to	Have Has Had	
paint			will / going to	Have Has Had	
pardon			will / going to	Have Has Had	
pray			will / going to	Have Has Had	
persuade			will / going to	Have Has Had	
prevent			will / going to	Have Has Had	
put			will / going to	Have Has Had	

I / we / you / they — have
he / she / it — has
I / we / you / they / he / she / it — had

FILL IN THE BLANKS

VERB: PAINT

	PAST	PRESENT	FUTURE
SIMPLE	+ed, new word, did not, did? (I,we,you,they)(he,she,it) 1. ____ _____ my room. 2. ____ __ __ _____ my room. 3. ____ ____ _____ my room?	verb, +s,es, do not, do? (I,we,you,they)(he,she,it) 1. ____ _____ may room. 2. ____ __ __ _____ my room. 3. ____ _____ _____ my room?	will, will not, will? (I,we,you,they)(he,she,it) 1. ____ _____ my room. 2. ____ ____ _____ my room. 3. ____ _____ _____ my room?
CONTINUOUS +ing = action continues for a time	was, were, +ing, not, ? (we,you,they)(I,he,she,it) 1. _____ _____ my room. 2. _____ _____ _____ my room. 3. _____ ____ _____ my room?	am,is,are, not, ? (I)(we,you,they)(he,she,it) 1. _____ _____ my room. 2. _____ ____ _____ my room. 3. _____ _____ _____ my room?	will be, will not be, will ? (we,you,they)(I,he,she,it) 1. _____ _____ my room. 2. _____ _____ _____ my room. 3. ___ ___ _____ my room?
PERFECT had,have,has,will have PP actions completed in past, but relates to another time	had, had PP, not PP, had PP? (we,you,they)(I,he,she,it) 1. ____ _____ my room. 2. _____ _____ _____ my room. 3. ___ _____ _____ my room?	have, has PP, not PP, PP? (I,we,you,they)(he,she,it) 1. _____ _____ my room. 2. _____ ____ _____ my room. 3. _____ _____ _____ my room?	will have PP, will not have PP, PP? (I,we,you,they)(he,she,it) 1. _____ _____ may room. 2. _____ _____ my room. 3. ____ _____ my room?
PERFECT CONTINUOUS +had,have,has been completed, but will continue	had been +ing, had not been +ing, Had __ +ing? (we,you,they)(I,he,she,it) 1. _____ _____ my room. 2. _____ _____ my room. 3. _____ _____ my room?	have, has been +ing, not been +ing, been +ing? (I,we,you,they)(he,she,it) 1. _____ _____ my room. 2. ____ ____ __ _____ my room. 3. ____ ____ _____ my room?	will have been +ing, will not, +ing? (I,we,you,they)(he,she,it) 1. ____ _____ my room. 2. _____ _____ my room. 3. _____ _____ my room?

MOVIE REVIEWS

      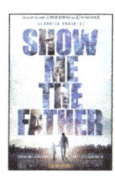  

Which movie is your favorite movie and why?

EXTRA

Write the premise of each movie. Who were the main characters, and what was the point of each movie.

Describe

Choose one movie and write a review.
Would you recommend it?
Why or why not?
What was the best part of the movie?
What could have been better
about the movie?

 **VOCABULARY**

Lesson 11

Heading to Rome

	- putting others first - serving and helping others	🔊

🏁	😭	⛵ ➡️

REVIEW WHAT YOU KNOW:

He has a bike. This is (her/his/theirs) bike.	
The opposite of true is _____.	
Plural of leaf.	
Punctuation for great emotion.	

Where is, are…	**Prefix re-**	

Things People Say

At weddings	At funerals	At hospitals	At work	At school

 **BIBLE**

Acts 20

The Bible says,

20:17 "Now from Miletus, he sent to Ephesus and called for the elders of the church.

20:18 And when they came to him, he said to them; "You know, from the first day I set foot in Asia, how I was with you the whole time-

20:19 serving the Lord with all humility, with tears, and with the trials (troubles) that came to me through the plots of the Jews -

20:20 and that I did not shrink back from proclaiming to you anything that was profitable or from teaching it to you in public and from house to house.

20:21 I testified to both Jews and Greeks about repentance toward God and faith in our Lord Jesus.

20:22 "And now I am on my way to Jerusalem, bound in my spirit, not knowing what I will encounter there,

20:23 except that in town after town the Holy Spirit testifies to me that chains and afflictions (troubles) are waiting for me.

20:24 But I count my life of no value to myself, so that I may finish my course and the ministry I received from the Lord Jesus, to testify to the gospel of God's grace.'

20:36 After he said this, he knelt down and prayed with all of them.

20:37 There was a great deal of weeping by everyone. They embraced Paul and kissed him,

20:38 grieving most of all over his statement that they would never see his face again. Then they escorted him to the ship." Acts 20:17-24;36-38HCSB

In your own words:

20:17-21 The Christians in Ephesus were very special to Paul. He served them and the Lord by_____

_____.

> **BIBLE**

Acts 23 and 27

The Bible says,
23:11 "The following night, the Lord stood by him and said, 'Have courage! For as you have testified about Me in Jerusalem, so you must also testify in Rome.'
27:1 When it was decided that we were to sail to Italy (Rome), they handed over Paul and some other prisoners to a centurion named Julius, of the Imperial Regiment.
27:9 By now much time had passed, and the voyage was already dangerous. Since the Fast was already over, Paul gave his advice
27:10 and told them, 'Men, I can see that this voyage is headed toward damage and heavy loss, not only of the cargo and the ship but also of our lives.'
27:11 But the centurion paid attention to the captain and the owner of the ship rather than to what Paul said.
27:20 For many days neither sun nor stars appeared, and the severe storm kept raging. Finally all hope that we would be saved was disappearing.
27:21 Since many were going without food, Paul stood up among them and said, 'You men should have followed my advice not to sail from Crete and sustain this damage and loss." Acts 23 and 27 HCSB

In your own words:
23:11 God came to encourage Paul and tell him that _____.
27:10-11 Paul knew what would happen, but _____.

BIBLE

Acts 27

The Bible says,

27:22 "'Now I urge you to take courage, because there will be no loss of any of your lives, but only of the ship.

27:23 For this night an angel of the God I belong to and serve stood by me,

27:24 and said, "Don't be afraid, Paul. You must stand before Caesar. And, look! God has graciously given you all those who are sailing with you.'

27:25 Therefore, take courage, men, because I believe God that it will be just the way it was told to me.

27:26 However, we must run aground on a certain island.'" Acts 27:22-26 HCSB

In your own words:

27:24 Paul listened to the message form God and believed Him. He told the other men on the boat that ___

_____.

27:26 Paul also told them that they were going to _____.

Application:

- Do you listen for God to speak to you? His Words to us are the Bible. Do you read it waiting to know what He is saying to you?
- Would you be as courageous and encouraging as Paul was in these circumstances?

LET'S TALK # Verb, Pronoun, and Contractions Practice

Circle the correct verb and answer the question using contractions in your answer.

1. Where (is / are) you?
2. Where (is / are) Matt and Melissa?
3. Where (is / are) you and Meg?
4. Where (is / are) Tim?
5. Where (is / are) the phone?
6. Where (is / are) the pencils?
7. Where (is / are) you going?
8. Where (is / are) you from?
9. Where (is / are) the chips?
10. Where (is / are) the teacher?
11. Where (is / are) you going?
12. Where (is / are) Molly and Inda?

Describe

WRITING

FILL IN THE BLANKS

Irregular Verbs & Past Participles

MAIN VERB	← PAST	↓ PRESENT	→ FUTURE	Have/Has/Had	PAST PARTICIPLE
qualify			will / going to	Have/Has/Had	
question			will / going to	Have/Has/Had	
read			will / going to	Have/Has/Had	
rebuild			will / going to	Have/Has/Had	
refer			will / going to	Have/Has/Had	
regret			will / going to	Have/Has/Had	
relax			will / going to	Have/Has/Had	
reply			will / going to	Have/Has/Had	
rewind			will / going to	Have/Has/Had	
ride			will / going to	Have/Has/Had	

I / we / you / they — have
he / she / it — has
I / we / you / they / he / she / it — had

FILL IN THE BLANKS	PAST	PRESENT	FUTURE
VERB: RIDE			

	PAST	PRESENT	FUTURE
SIMPLE	+ed,new word, did not, did? (I,we,you,they)(he,she,it) 1. ____ _____ the bus. 2. ____ ____ _____ the bus. 3. ____ ____ _____ the bus?	verb, +s,es,do not, do? (I,we,you,they)(he,she,it) 1. ____ _____ the bus. 2. _____ ____ _____ the bus. 3. ____ _____ _____ the bus?	will, will not, will? (I,we,you,they)(he,she,it) 1. _____ _____ the bus. 2. _____ ____ _____ the bus. 3. _____ _____ _____ the bus?
CONTINUOUS +ing = action continues for a time	was, were, +ing, not, ? (we,you,they)(I,he,she,it) 1. _____ _____ the bus. 2. ____ ____ _____ the bus. 3. _____ ____ _____ the bus?	am,is,are, not, ? (I)(we,you,they)(he,she,it) 1. _____ _____ the bus. 2. _____ ____ _____ the bus. 3. ____ _____ _____ the bus?	will be, will not be, will ? (we,you,they)(I,he,she,it) 1. _____ _____ the bus. 2. _____ ____ _____ the bus. 3. ____ ____ _____ the bus?
PERFECT had,have,has,will have PP actions completed in past, but relates to another time	had, had PP, not PP, had PP? (we,you,they)(I,he,she,it) 1. ____ ____ _____ the bus. 2. ____ ____ ___ _____ the bus. 3. ___ _____ _____ the bus?	have, has PP, not PP, PP? (I,we,you,they)(he,she,it) 1. _____ ____ _____ the bus. 2. ____ ____ ____ _____ the bus. 3. _____ _____ _____ the bus?	will have PP, will not have PP, PP? (I,we,you,they)(he,she,it) 1._____ _____ _____ the bus. 2. _____ _____ the bus. 3. _____ _____ the bus?
PERFECT CONTINUOUS +had,have,has been completed, but will continue	had been +ing, had not been +ing, Had __ +ing? (we,you,they)(I,he,she,it) 1. _____ _____ the bus. 2. _____ _____ the bus. 3. _____ _____ _____ the bus?	have, has been +ing, not been +ing, been +ing? (I,we,you,they)(he,she,it) 1. _____ _____ the bus. 2. ____ ____ _____ the bus. 3. _____ _____ the bus?	will have been +ing, will not, +ing? (I,we,you,they)(he,she,it) 1. _____ _____ the bus. 2._____ _____ the bus. 3. ____ _____ _____ the bus?

EXTRA

MAKE A MOVIE

Write down your movie ideas. If you were a movie writer, what movie would you make?

Theme:
Characters:
Setting:
Problem / Solution:
Movie Title:

 **EXTRA**

Draw your movie marquee.

Describe the elements in your marquee and why you included them.

VOCABULARY

Lesson 12

Shipwrecked

REVIEW WHAT YOU KNOW:

Poisonous		Yes, you may.

We have a lot of books we will _____.	
forty-three minus twelve equals ?	
Past, Present, Future of "see."	
Have you ever _____ an electric car?	

- months in a year - days in a year - days in a week	twenty twenty-two nineteen eighty-five fourteen ninety-two	

VOCABULARY

During the Months

January	February	March	April	May	June

July	August	September	October	November	December

| BIBLE | Acts 28 |

The Bible says, that the ship wrecked, but everyone swam shore safely just like God told Paul.
28:1 "Once ashore, we then learned that the island was called Malta.
28:2 The local people showed us extraordinary kindness, for they lit a fire and took us all in, since it was raining and cold.
28:3 As Paul gathered a bundle of brushwood and put it on the fire, a viper came out because of the heat and fastened itself to his hand (bit him).
28:4 When the local people saw the creature hanging from his hand, they said to one another, 'This man is probably a murderer, and though he has escaped the sea, Justice does not allow him to live!'
28:5 However, he shook the creature off into the fire and suffered no harm.
28:6 They expected that he would well up or suddenly drop dead. But after they waited a long time and saw nothing unusual happen to him, they changed their minds and said he was a god." Acts 28:1-6HCSB

In your own words:
28:2 The people of the island _____.
28:3 The poisonous snake _____.
28:5 Paul _____.

BIBLE   # Acts 28

The Bible says,
28:11 "After three months we set sail in an Alexandrian ship that had wintered at the island….
28:12 Putting in at Syracuse, we stayed three days.
28:13 From there, after making a circuit along the coast, we reached Rhenium. After one day a south wind sprang up, and the second day we came to Puteoli.
28:14 There we found believers and were invited to stay with them for seven days. And so we came to Rome.
28:15 Now the believers from there had heard the news about us and had come to meet us as far as the Forum of Appius and the Three Taverns. When Paul saw them, he thanked God and took courage.
28:16 When we entered Rome, Paul was permitted to stay by himself with the soldier who guarded him."
Acts 28:11-16 HCSB

In your own words:
28:14-15 Paul wrote the letter of Romans to the believers in Rome. The letter had been sent there before he came. When Paul met the believers he _____.
28:16 The Romans let Paul _____.

`BIBLE`   # Acts 28

The Bible says,
28:30 "Then he stayed two whole years in his own rented house. And he welcomed all who visited him,
28:31 proclaiming the kingdom of God and teaching the things concerning the Lord Jesus Christ with full boldness and without hindrance." Acts 28:30-31HCSB

In your own words:
28:30-31 Paul was able to teach and preach while under arrest (even living in his own home), so he _____.

Application:
- Many of the other books of the Bible are letters that Paul wrote while he was in prison in Rome. These letters were written to churches, to individuals, to believers telling them how to follow Jesus well.
- What is the most interesting thing you learned reading these stories in Acts?
- How can you be a witness like this?

LET'S TALK　　# Past Tense with past participles

Follow the example in #1 to complete the sentences.

1. It is time for the National Anthem? No, it has already been sung.

2. Do I need to hide the present? No, it is already _____.

3. Should I write all of the names? No, they have been _____.

4. Do you want me to do the laundry? No, it has already been _____.

5 Are the visitors still here? No, they are already _____.

6. Do I need to take out the trash? No, it has already been _____.

7. Should I feed the dogs? No, they have been _____.

8. I was going to send the packages, but they have already been _____.

9. Do you want me to set the alarm? No, it has already been _____.

10. Should I clean the bathroom? No, it has been _____ already.

11. Do you want him to hang up the signs? No, they have already been _____.

12. Do I need to give out the letters? No, they have already been _____.

WRITING

Describe

FILL IN THE BLANKS

Irregular Verbs & Past Participles

MAIN VERB	← PAST	↓ PRESENT	→ FUTURE	Have Has Had	PAST PARTICIPLE
say			will / going to	Have Has Had	
see			will / going to	Have Has Had	
sell			will / going to	Have Has Had	
send			will / going to	Have Has Had	
shut			will / going to	Have Has Had	
sing			will / going to	Have Has Had	
sit			will / going to	Have Has Had	
sleep			will / going to	Have Has Had	
speak			will / going to	Have Has Had	
spend			will / going to	Have Has Had	

I we you they — have

he she it — has

I we you they he she it — had

FILL IN THE BLANKS

VERB: SEE

	PAST	PRESENT	FUTURE
SIMPLE	+ed, new word, did not, did? (I,we,you,they)(he,she,it) 1. ____ _____ the stars. 2. ___ ____ ___ _____ the stars. 3. ___ ____ _____ the stars?	verb, +s,es, do not, do? (I,we,you,they)(he,she,it) 1. ____ _____ the stars. 2. ____ ____ ___ _____ the stars 3. ____ ____ _____ the stars?	will, will not, will? (I,we,you,they)(he,she,it) 1. ____ ____ _____ the stars. 2. ____ ____ ___ _____ the stars. 3. ____ ____ _____ the stars?
CONTINUOUS +ing = action continues for a time	was, were, +ing, not, ? (we,you,they)(I,he,she,it) 1. ____ ____ _____ the stars 2. ____ ____ ___ _____ the stars. 3. ____ ____ _____ the stars?	am, is, are, not, ? (I)(we,you,they)(he,she,it) 1. ____ ____ _____ the stars. 2. ____ ____ ___ _____ the stars. 3. ____ ____ _____ the stars?	will be, will not be, will ? (we,you,they)(I,he,she,it) 1. ____ ____ _____ the stars. 2. ____ ____ _____ the stars. 3. ____ ____ _____ the stars?
PERFECT had,have,has,will have PP actions completed in past, but relates to another time	had, had PP, not PP, had PP? (we,you,they)(I,he,she,it) 1. ____ ____ _____ the stars. 2. ____ ____ ___ _____ the stars. 3. ____ ____ _____ the stars?	have, has PP, not PP, PP? (I,we,you,they)(he,she,it) 1. ____ ____ _____ the stars. 2. ____ ____ ___ _____ the stars. 3. ____ ____ _____ the stars?	will have PP, will not have PP, PP? (I,we,you,they)(he,she,it) 1. ____ ____ _____ the stars. 2. ____ ____ _____ the stars. 3. ____ ____ _____ the stars?
PERFECT CONTINUOUS +had,have,has been completed, but will continue	had been +ing, had not been +ing, Had __ +ing? (we,you,they)(I,he,she,it) 1. ____ ____ _____ the stars. 2. ____ ____ _____ the stars. 3. ____ ____ _____ the stars?	have, has been +ing, not been +ing, been +ing? (I,we,you,they)(he,she,it) 1. ____ ____ _____ the stars. 2. ____ ____ _____ the stars. 3. ____ ____ _____ the stars?	will have been +ing, will not, +ing? (I,we,you,they)(he,she,it) 1. ____ ____ _____ the stars. 2. ____ ____ _____ the stars. 3. ____ ____ _____ the stars?

EXTRA HOMEWORK: Watch the movie *Lifemark.*
Set the subtitles to your language so you can
understand the story.

Movie Review Questions:

Write your own questions that you can ask the other students in class to see what they remember from the movie.
Question One:
Question Two:
Question Three:

Lesson 13 — The Roman Road

	God's fame / God's honor	payment	
	1+2=3 What happened		

REVIEW WHAT YOU KNOW:

Favorite English Word	
Hardest English word to say	
Favorite Bible story	
Favorite Bible verse	

doesn't follow the grammar rules	given, taken, seen, shown, forgiven, chosen	

`BIBLE`

Romans

In this letter that Paul wrote to the people in Rome, the Bible says,

3:23 "For all have sinned and fall short of the glory of God."

5:8 "But God proves His own love for us in that while we were still sinners, Christ died for us!"

6:23 "For the wages of sin is death, but the gift of God is eternal life in Christ Jesus our Lord."

10:9-10 "If you confess with your mouth, 'Jesus is Lord,' and believe in your heart that God raised Him from the dead, you will be saved. One believes with the heart, resulting in righteousness, and one confesses with the mouth, resulting in salvation."

In your own words:

3:23 Everyone _____.

5:8 God showed His love by _____.

6:23 The payment for sin is _____ but _____.

10:9-10 The way to be saved is _____.

We call these verses in Romans the Roman Road because they explain the way to be saved.

Application:

- Have you ever understood that you need to be saved from your sins?
- Have you ever thought about how amazing that even in your sin, God sent Jesus to die for you?
- Do you know that your sin causes spiritual death that means going to Hell, but God offers the free gift of spiritual life (Heaven)?
- Have you confessed that you believe "Jesus is Lord"?

LET'S TALK # Past Tense with Past Participles

Follow the example in #1 to complete the sentences.

1. They gave him an award - That's the second time he <u>has been given</u> an award.

2. They took her to the hospital - That's the fifth time she _____ to the hospital.

3. They sent her to New York - That's the second time she _____ to New York

4. They offered her a contract - That's the third time she _____ a contract.

5. They chose him as teacher of the year - That's the second time he _____ as teacher of the year.

6. They invited the family over - That's the third time this week the family _____ over.

WRITING

Describe

136

FILL IN THE BLANKS — Irregular Verbs & Past Participles

MAIN VERB	← PAST	↓ PRESENT	→ FUTURE	Have/Has/Had PAST PARTICIPLE
take			will / going to	Have/Has/Had
tap			will / going to	Have/Has/Had
tear			will / going to	Have/Has/Had
think			will / going to	Have/Has/Had
throw			will / going to	Have/Has/Had
tell			will / going to	Have/Has/Had
thank			will / going to	Have/Has/Had
translate			will / going to	Have/Has/Had
try			will / going to	Have/Has/Had
use			will / going to	Have/Has/Had

I, we, you, they — have
he, she, it — has
I, we, you, they, he, she, it — had

FILL IN THE BLANKS

Irregular Verbs & Past Participles

MAIN VERB	← PAST	↓ PRESENT	→ FUTURE	Have Has Had	PAST PARTICIPLE
wake			will / going to	Have Has Had	
wear			will / going to	Have Has Had	
win			will / going to	Have Has Had	
worry			will / going to	Have Has Had	
write			will / going to	Have Has Had	
wave			will / going to	Have Has Had	
wish			will / going to	Have Has Had	
welcome			will / going to	Have Has Had	
yield			will / going to	Have Has Had	
yawn			will / going to	Have Has Had	

I
we
you
they   have

he
she
it   has

I
we
you
they

he
she
it   had

FILL IN THE BLANKS

VERB: TAKE

	PAST	PRESENT	FUTURE
SIMPLE	+ed, new word, did not, did? (I,we,you,they)(he,she,it) 1. ____ _____ a nap. 2. ___ ___ ___ _____ a nap. 3. ___ ___ _____ a nap?	verb, +s,es, do not, do? (I,we,you,they)(he,she,it) 1. ____ _____ a nap. 2. ___ ___ ___ _____ a nap 3. ___ ____ ____ a nap?	will, will not, will? (I,we,you,they)(he,she,it) 1. ____ _____ a nap. 2. ___ ____ ___ _____ a nap. 3. ___ ____ ____ a nap?
CONTINUOUS +ing = action continues for a time	was, were, +ing, not, ? (we,you,they)(I,he,she,it) 1. ____ ____ _____ a nap. 2. ___ ___ _ _____ a nap. 3. ___ ____ ____ a nap?	am, is, are, not, ? (I)(we,you,they)(he,she,it) 1. ____ ____ _____ a nap. 2. ___ ___ ___ _____ a nap. 3. ___ ____ ____ a nap?	will be, will not be, will ? (we,you,they)(I,he,she,it) 1. ____ ____ _____ a nap. 2. ___ ____ ___ _____ a nap. 3. ___ ____ ____ a nap?
PERFECT had, have, has, will have PP actions completed in past, but relates to another time	had, had PP, not PP, had PP? (we,you,they)(I,he,she,it) 1. ____ ____ ____ a nap. 2. ___ ____ ___ _____ a nap. 3. ___ ____ ____ a nap?	have, has PP, not PP, PP? (I,we,you,they)(he,she,it) 1. ____ ____ ____ a nap. 2. ___ ____ ___ _____ a nap. 3. ___ ____ ____ a nap?	will have PP, will not have PP, PP? (I,we,you,they)(he,she,it) 1. _____ _____ a nap. 2. ___ ____ ____ _____ a nap. 3. ___ ____ _____ a nap?
PERFECT CONTINUOUS +had, have, has been completed, but will continue	had been +ing, had not been +ing, Had __ +ing? (we,you,they)(I,he,she,it) 1. ____ ____ ____ _____ a nap. 2. ___ ___ ___ ___ _____ _____ a nap. 3. ___ ____ ____ _____ a nap?	have, has been +ing, not been +ing, been +ing? (I,we,you,they)(he,she,it) 1. ____ ____ ____ _____ a nap. 2. ___ ___ ___ _____ _____ a nap. 3. ___ ____ ____ _____ a nap?	will have been +ing, will not, +ing? (I,we,you,they)(he,she,it) 1. ____ ____ ____ _____ a nap. 2. ___ ____ ____ _____ _____ a nap. 3. ___ ____ _____ _____ a nap?

FILL IN THE BLANKS

VERB: WRITE

	PAST	PRESENT	FUTURE
SIMPLE	+ed,new word, did not, did? (I,we,you,they)(he,she,it) 1. _____ _____ a note. 2. ___ ____ ___ ____ a note. 3. ___ ____ _____ a note?	verb, +s,es,do not, do? (I,we,you,they)(he,she,it) 1. ____ _____ a note. 2. ___ ____ ___ _____ a note 3. _____ _____ _____ a note?	will, will not, will? (I,we,you,they)(he,she,it) 1. _____ _____ a note. 2. _____ ____ _____ a note. 3. ___ _____ ____ a note?
CONTINUOUS +ing = action continues for a time	was, were, +ing, not, ? (we,you,they)(I,he,she,it) 1. _____ _____ a note. 2. ____ ____ ____ _____ a note. 3. ____ ____ _____ a note?	am,is,are, not, ? (I)(we,you,they)(he,she,it) 1. _____ _____ a note. 2. ____ ____ ___ _____ a note. 3. ____ ____ _____ a note?	will be, will not be, will ? (we,you,they)(I,he,she,it) 1. ____ _____ a note. 2._____ ____ ____ a note. 3. ___ ____ _____ a note?
PERFECT had,have,has,will have PP actions completed in past, but relates to another time	had, had PP, not PP, had PP? (we,you,they)(I,he,she,it) 1.____ ____ ____ a note. 2.____ ____ ___ _____ a note. 3. ___ ____ ____ a note?	have, has PP, not PP, PP? (I,we,you,they)(he,she,it) 1. _____ ____ _____ a note. 2. ____ ___ ___ _____ a note. 3. ____ _____ _____ a note?	will have PP, will not have PP, PP? (I,we,you,they)(he,she,it) 1._____ _____ _____ a note. 2.____ ____ ____ _____ a note. 3.____ _____ _____ a note?
PERFECT CONTINUOUS +had,have,has been completed, but will continue	had been +ing, had not been +ing, Had __ +ing? (we,you,they)(I,he,she,it) 1. _____ _____ ____ _____ a note. 2. _____ ____ ____ _____ _____ a note. 3. ____ ____ ____ _____ a note?	have, has been +ing, not been +ing, been +ing? (I,we,you,they)(he,she,it) 1. _____ ____ _____ _____ a note. 2. ____ ____ ___ ____ _____ a note. 3. _____ ____ ____ _____ a note?	will have been +ing, will not, +ing? (I,we,you,they)(he,she,it) 1. ____ _____ ____ _____ a note. 2.____ ____ ____ ____ a note. 3. ___ _____ _____ _____ a note?

CONGRATULATIONS

Level 1 - Completed
Level 2 - Completed
Level 3 - Completed
Level 4 - Completed
Level 5

Go to www.TexasBibleEnglish.com for level 5 books and videos.

Look for our kids' book series called: Texas Bible Kids

Amazon link: https://a.co/d/cNUAkQC   Amazon link: https://a.co/d/6B0zhdg